I0754887

CHASING ERUPTIONS

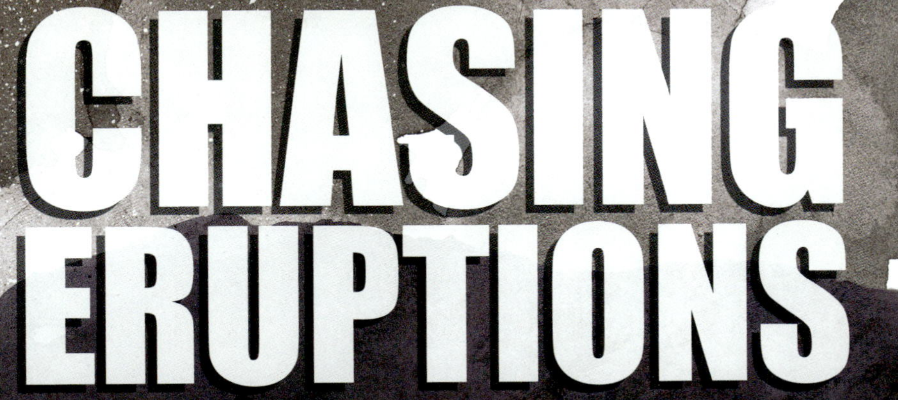

CHASING ERUPTIONS

How Volcanologists Maurice and Katia Krafft Helped Save 60,000 Lives—But Lost Their Own

CURTIS MANLEY

Illustrated by Katherine Roy

CLARION BOOKS
An Imprint of HarperCollinsPublishers

HarperCollins Children's Books, a division of
HarperCollins Publishers, 195 Broadway, New York, NY 10007
HarperCollins Publishers, Macken House,
39/40 Mayor Street Upper, Dublin 1, D01 C9W8, Ireland

Clarion Books is an imprint of HarperCollins Publishers.

Chasing Eruptions

Manufactured in Grude, Bosnia and Herzegovina.

harpercollins.com

Library of Congress Control Number: 2025943579
ISBN 978-0-06-338629-7

Book design by Alison Klapthor
26 27 28 29 30 GPS 10 9 8 7 6 5 4 3 2 1

First Edition

To Katia & Maurice
and all who follow their own passions
and bring discovery, empathy,
and beauty to the world.
—Curtis Manley

To my Dad,
who sparked my love of art and science
and taught me to follow where curiosity leads.
—Katherine Roy

Volcanoes and Volcanic Areas Visited by the Kraffts

MAP KEY

- ■ The Alsace region of northeastern France, where Maurice and Katia were born and lived
- ○ Volcanoes mentioned in this book
- ● Some of the other volcanoes visited by the Kraffts
- ▲ La Cité du Volcan interpretive center and Vulcania theme park the Kraffts helped create

CONTENTS

The Last Day

Mount Unzen, Japan

June 3, 1991, 4:08 p.m.

"Risk is the very engine of life. . . . if you don't take risks . . .
you've missed out on your own life."
—Maurice Krafft

As the brown ash flow
moved down the mountain,
swelling up, hiding the volcano,
and blotting out the sky,
it came closer and closer
to where they stood.

Maurice and Katia Krafft
knew that ash flows like this
were much hotter than fire
and moved much faster
than anyone could run.

They had watched other flows
earlier that day, watched them
from the start, as great blocks
broke off the hot lava dome
at the summit of the mountain
and shattered into boulders.

As those boulders began to roll
they shattered again and again,
disappearing behind a mass of dust
that rushed faster and faster down the slope,
directly toward Maurice and Katia.
But then, at the last moment,
each flow had turned
to follow the valley
of the Mizunashi River.

Compared to the flows
from earlier that day,
this one had grown much larger.
So large, they knew
that only some of it
would turn safely away.

So large, they surely knew
they could not escape it.

In the short time
before the flow reached them,
did Katia and Maurice look back
over the events in their lives
that had brought them
to this moment
on Unzen?

Young Katia

Alsace, Eastern France

1942–57

When she was born she was named
Catherine Marie Joséphine Conrad—
but no one called her that.
It was always just
Katia.

Like many children,
Katia was fascinated by pebbles—

their shapes and colors and textures.
She asked question after question
until her mother ran out of answers.

When she was eleven, she told a friend
she would be a volcanologist—
but she did not tell her parents.

When Katia was a young teen, she and her family
explored the extinct cinder cones, lava domes,
and sparkling crater lakes
of the Chaîne des Puys
in the Auvergne region of central France.
After that trip, she spoke out loud
what she'd decided years before:
She wanted to be a scientist.

But her parents expected Katia to teach school,
just like her mother. So when she was fifteen,
Katia began training to become a teacher.

Her dream of studying volcanoes
seemed as far away as their cloudy peaks.

Young Maurice

Alsace, Eastern France

1946–59

*"The earth has always interested me.
Some days I lived in the dinosaur era; other days
I was with the trilobites. I was crazy about that as a kid."
—Maurice*

Maurice Paul Krafft
was born just thirteen miles
from where Katia lived.

When he was seven years old,
his family vacationed in Italy
to visit Mount Etna
and the volcanic islands nearby.

In the great crater on Vulcano
they saw steaming vents called fumaroles,
crusted orange and yellow from sulfur.

On Lipari they gathered pumice stones
and floated them on the waves
like tiny boats on a restless sea.

One night on Stromboli, Maurice and his father
hiked three hours to the summit
and looked down into the craters.
Glowing bits of molten lava exploded into the sky
and lit up the dark like fireworks.
BOOM!
BOOM!
The sharp smell of sulfur filled each breath
and clung to their clothes.
BOOM!

Like catching a fever that never goes away,
Maurice had caught volcanoes.

Even the death and destruction he saw
when his family visited the ruins of Pompeii,
buried by an eruption of Mount Vesuvius,
didn't cool that fever.

When Maurice returned home,
it was Stromboli he thought about most.
He scooped sand into mounds
and blew them up with firecrackers,
watching the sand spray up and out,
covering the ground in all directions
and leaving empty craters.

He began collecting rocks and minerals,
and by the time he was fourteen
he knew more about them
than his teachers did—
and he didn't hesitate to say so.
Like the time a teacher
held up a sample
and said it was limestone.
Maurice knew it wasn't.
He took the rock and scratched
the classroom window—
something that limestone
is too soft to do . . .

Maurice's best friend at school, Roland,
was also interested in rocks.
And soon, because Maurice
talked about volcanoes all the time,
Roland caught volcanoes too.

Stromboli is a small, volcanic Italian island known as "the lighthouse of the Mediterranean" because it has erupted almost continuously for thousands of years.

Pompeii was an ancient Roman city just five miles from the base of Mount Vesuvius. Its soils were rich and fertile due to the ash of long-forgotten eruptions. But then in 79 AD, Vesuvius erupted again. A column of ash rose so high that it blotted out the sun. Pumice stones fell from the sky for hours, collapsing the roofs of houses and filling the streets. Thousands of people fled the city, but some stayed behind thinking the worst was over. And then ash flows swept down the volcano's slopes, igniting anything in their path and filling buildings with hot gases and scorching ash. No one who stayed in the city survived, but they are all still there: The buried bodies decayed away, leaving hollows in the ash where they had been. When archaeologists discovered the hollows, they poured in plaster, creating 3D molds. Visitors to the ruins of Pompeii can see the white shapes of adults, children, and a dog who all died when the ash flows rushed into the city nearly two thousand years ago.

Katia and the Wall of Death

Alsace, Eastern France

August 1957

Even if she would become
a teacher like her mother,
Katia
was not really like her at all.

Every year at the end of August
the carnival came to town.
There were bumper cars and candy sellers,
and if you were lucky
you might win a chicken
or rabbit or a pair of pigeons.

But the year Katia turned fifteen,
there was something new:
the Wall of Death.
It was a wire cage
in the shape of a tall cylinder,
and inside were stuntmen
driving fast in motorcycles
and a tiny Vespa car.
They went around and around
sideways
clinging to the curved wall

like quick, buzzing insects.
Katia's family and uncles and aunts
were spellbound.

When the show was over
the adults walked home and let the kids
stay longer at the carnival.
No one else noticed when Katia
returned home, talked with her father,
and went back with him
to the Wall of Death.

The stuntmen
had offered her a free ride
as a passenger in the Vespa car
to entice others to pay—
but she needed a parent's permission.
Katia's mother was the school principal
in a town so small that everyone
knew everyone else;
she would never agree
to anything like that!
So Katia and her father kept it a secret
from the others at home.

The next day at the market
her mother was stunned
when the sellers and other shoppers

congratulated her
about how very brave Katia had been,
riding in that tiny car,
around and around
sideways.

Their Dreams on the Screen

Alsace, Eastern France

1959

In different theaters,
in towns just a few miles apart,
Katia and Maurice each saw the same film:
Les Rendez-vous du diable—
or, in English, "Meetings with the Devil"—
by the famous filmmaker volcanologist
Haroun Tazieff.

They watched as Tazieff and his team . . .
Climbed forbidden volcanoes!
Descended on ropes into the deepest craters!
Explored lakes of bubbling lava!
Braved fountains of fire!
Sampled molten rock!
Measured the heat of the Earth!

That was what Katia longed to do.

That was the life Maurice dreamed of.

Katia, Teaching

Alsace, Eastern France

1960–61

"Once you see an eruption, you can't live without it,
because it's so big, it's so strong."
—Katia

When she was eighteen,
Katia finished her teacher training
after three long years—
and vacationed with her family in Italy.

They spent two days in awe
at rivers of red flowing lava on Mount Etna,
the biggest volcano in Europe, and at sunset
they watched Etna cast its purple shadow
into the far distance, over the darkened waves
of the Mediterranean.

Like Maurice before,
Katia and her family climbed Stromboli,
where the lava fireworks
lit up the night—
and lit up Katia's dazzled face.

After they returned home,
Katia began teaching math and science
to middle school students. Her mother
was so proud of her, but Katia
was miserable.

After a year, she asked her parents
to let her learn geochemistry
at the nearby University of Strasbourg.

Finally, they said *Yes*.

Geochemistry is the study of chemical reactions among the materials of the Earth—minerals, waters, and gases. Water is necessary for some minerals to form, but it can cause other minerals to dissolve or break down. The chemical composition of volcanic gases can show how hot they were before they rose to the Earth's surface and cooled—and might reveal whether new magma is present and the depth it came from.

Maurice and Friends

France

1962–66

When he was just fifteen years old
Maurice became a member
of the Geological Society of France—
the youngest person to ever
be allowed to join.

That same year Maurice and Roland
led their friends on a 250-mile moped trip
to explore the extinct volcanoes
of the Chaîne des Puys
in central France.

To continue studying geology,
Maurice enrolled at the University of Strasbourg.
And Roland did, too.

That first year at the university,
dreams came true for Maurice and Roland.
They met Haroun Tazieff in Italy
and joined him and his team for eight days
of watching eruptions on Mount Etna!
Tazieff said he was impressed with them,

told them to study volcanology,
and offered to help with their careers.

And he said if they truly wanted
to learn about volcanoes,
they must visit
Iceland.

Geology is the study of Earth. Geologists study Earth's minerals, rocks, and internal structure; mountains and other landforms; and lakes, rivers, and oceans. They hope to understand the formation and history of the Earth, the movements of the tectonic plates, the origin of mineral deposits, and the variety and evolution of life.

Volcanology is the study of volcanoes. Volcanologists are geologists who study volcanoes, the movement of magma (molten rock while still underground), eruptions, and the rock and ash produced when magma reaches the surface (and is then called lava). They hope to understand how different kinds of volcanoes work, what the warning signs of eruptions might be, and the hazards that volcanoes pose for those people who live or work on or near them.

Maurice and Katia

Strasbourg, Alsace, Eastern France

1966

Taking Tazieff's advice, Maurice and Roland
began planning a trip to Iceland.
They wanted to make short movies there,
like the films of Tazieff and his team.
So Roland told Maurice about another student
whose grandfather would give her money
if she wanted to buy a movie camera—
and who talked about volcanoes
all the time. Roland thought Maurice
should meet her!

The café near the university was busy.
Seated at a table, Maurice watched
for a small woman with big glasses.
Katia walked in the door and looked
for a tall man with curly brown hair.

They found each other and talked for hours.
Talked until the café closed for the night.
Then talked more as they walked together
along the dark streets of Strasbourg
in the rain.

First Expedition
Iceland

June–September 1968

Maurice, Katia, and Roland
agreed to work together as a team
of volcanologists. They called themselves
"L'Équipe Vulcain"—the Vulcan Team—
named after the god of fire in old Roman myths.
And they began wearing red knit caps,
just like Jacques Cousteau, who was famous
for diving beneath the waves to explore the sea.

They couldn't learn new things about volcanoes
just from reading books. They needed to go in person
to see, hear, and smell volcanoes. To climb them
and feel the little earthquakes beneath their feet.

But they had no money to go far from home—
until Maurice received travel grants
from a mining company
and the local government.
Then they were given a new car
as part of an advertising campaign
that featured explorers. Another business
gave them a trailer for their gear.

To Iceland, at last!
Getting there required a sea voyage—
so the car and trailer were loaded
onto a big cargo ship in Denmark.

Once the three of them reached Iceland,
they drove all the way around the island:
eight thousand miles on gravel roads, on dirt roads,
over dry deserts, and through cold, rushing rivers,
far from towns or people. They marveled
at the variety of volcanic landforms:
lava flows, long chains of craters, calderas,
ancient, flat-topped mountains formed under ice sheets,
and tall volcanoes hidden under glaciers.
They measured the temperatures
of hot springs and geysers
and collected gas samples from fumaroles.

But some things did not go well:
Maurice stepped in a hot spring and burned his leg,
Roland's kneecap was broken in a car crash,
they were swarmed by thick clouds of black flies,
the car got stuck in powdery ash
twenty-seven times in a row,
they lost rock samples and food when their trailer
was swept downstream in a flood,
and they were trapped for two days in the car
in the middle of an icy river.

When they returned home after three wonderful
and difficult months in what Katia called
"the paradise of volcanologists,"
the local newspaper printed a story
about their expedition.
Then, using their movie footage
and photographs,
they created their first short film
to share their love of volcanoes
with the world.

Iceland is an island built completely by volcanoes. It is a land of ice and fire, black lava and green moss, surrounded by the cold northern Atlantic Ocean. The volcanoes are active, but seem asleep under thick blankets of snow. When they wake up, ice melts and floods burst from beneath the glaciers. Volcanism in Iceland is fed by a plume of hot rock that starts near the Earth's core and rises slowly through the mantle, melting to create magma only when it gets near the surface. A similar mantle plume is also responsible for the volcanism in the Hawaiian islands. But unlike Hawai'i, Iceland is also part of the mid-Atlantic ridge, where the seafloor spreads apart, widening the Atlantic Ocean (and Iceland) and moving Europe and North America about one and a half inches farther apart each year.

On TV
Paris, France

September 1969

The French TV show *Meetings with Adventure*
invited the Vulcan Team to talk about volcanoes.
The show also invited Haroun Tazieff,
the volcanologist filmmaker they all admired
and who Maurice and Roland
had worked with on Etna.
They felt he was their friend.

Maurice, Katia, and Roland answered questions,
and Maurice showed clips of their Iceland film
while talking about the expedition.
Maurice smiled. He spoke easily, told stories,
and joked about their mishaps.
His personality filled the TV studio
and the rooms of all the viewers at home.

The host of the show
barely asked Tazieff any questions.
The younger volcanologists
got all the attention. Tazieff
was furious. He never again
offered them help
or advice.

Katia and the Gas Analyzer

Paris, France, and Vulcano, Italy

December 1969

Katia spent much of 1969
working with other chemists
to help design and build
the world's first gas analyzer
small enough to be carried onto a volcano
to measure different types of gases.

To test the new analyzer,
Katia and the Vulcan Team
traveled to the island of Vulcano,
off the coast of Sicily.
It took the three of them
to carry the analyzer—
and the two heavy car batteries
it needed for power—
up to the great crater.
Surrounded by tourists,
some of whom still wore
their swimsuits from the beach,
Katia sampled the steamy gases
drifting from the smelly,
sulfur-encrusted fumaroles
on the crater's rim.

The tests were a success!
Right there on the volcano
the analyzer determined which gases
were puffing out of the fumaroles
and how much of each gas there was.
This meant the samples
didn't need to be taken to a laboratory
hundreds or thousands of miles away.
And since a gas sample can change
after it's collected, analyzing it right away
gives more accurate results.

For her work, Katia won a prestigious
Vocation Prize, presented to her
by the French prime minister himself.

Honeymoon on a Volcano

Santorini, Greece

August 1970

Even if Katia and Maurice
had wanted a fancy wedding,
they didn't have the money for that.
And even if they'd had the money,
they would rather have spent it
to see volcanoes.
So their wedding was small,
with his parents and her parents
and a few relatives and friends.
Afterward, Maurice and Katia
left for a honeymoon . . .
on a volcano, of course!

The Greek island of Santorini
is shaped like a crescent moon,
its hollow center a volcanic caldera
where older peaks
exploded and collapsed
and allowed the sea to flow in.
The most recent big event
was the great Minoan eruption
3,600 years ago,
when the island was buried

under layer after layer of pumice
before the center blew itself apart,
leaving tall, steep cliffs
where the rest of the island
had been.

Maurice and Katia
stayed at the top of those cliffs,
in the bright white buildings
of the town of Firá,
and each evening
they watched the sun set
over the young lava islands
that had begun to fill the watery caldera.

From the base of the tall cliffs
they took a boat to the youngest
of those rocky islands.
Its most recent lava flows
were twenty years old,
but still warm and steaming—
and the yellowish-green water
of the hot springs was lovely to swim in.
They returned to town by riding the donkeys
hundreds of steps up the zigzag stairs
to the top of the cliffs.

They also visited the new diggings
near the town of Akrotiri,
where buildings up to three stories high
had been found under the pumice
of the great eruption—ancient houses,
workshops, and storerooms
where people had worked and lived
before the island had blown itself apart.

Inside the houses were cups, bowls,
pitchers, baking pans, storage jars,
and stones for grinding grain—
and colorful wall paintings
beautifully preserved
for thousands of years
since the eruption.

And there were hollows
where wooden beds, stools,
and tables had rotted away
after all those years
under layers of ash.
Just like at Pompeii, archaeologists
had poured plaster in
to reveal their original shapes
and decorations.

But there was something
that the archaeologists didn't find,
even though they looked carefully
inside all the rooms
and in the streets between houses.

Bodies.

If no hollows from bodies—
and no bones—
could be found, it must mean
that everyone had left
before
the great eruption.
Perhaps earthquakes
or the first small eruptions
had convinced those in Akrotiri
to abandon their homes
and escape in boats
to the safety of other islands.

But did they truly find safety
on those other islands—
or did the tsunami waves
of the great eruption
find them?
No one knows.

When Maurice and Katia left Santorini
they traveled on to Vulcano
to join the rest of the Vulcan Team,
which now had three new members.

They wanted to make more tests
with the gas analyzer—
and try out a new way
to measure the temperatures
of fumaroles.

And it would also be practice
for their next big mission . . .

The Lake of Acid

Indonesia

May–December 1971

The government of Indonesia
and the United Nations
asked the Vulcan Team to determine
which of Indonesia's volcanoes
might provide geothermal energy—
and which were the most dangerous.

For a project this big,
the team needed to be big as well.
Joining Maurice, Katia, and Roland
were Jean-Guy, Michel, and Gilbert.

Katia worked out the details: The team
would visit 39 of Indonesia's 127 active volcanoes.
It would take seven months, and they would need
lots of equipment: the car they had used in Iceland,
a big truck, containers for samples, helmets,
gas masks, heat-resistant clothing, gloves, boots . . .
And Maurice wanted a dependable rubber raft.
He found a used one at a flea market in France;
it had leaked, but the holes had been patched.
He thought it looked okay.

Katia was unimpressed.

She did not like Maurice's plan to float the raft
on the turquoise acid lake of Java's Kawah Ijen volcano.
She'd brought a piece of limestone from France,
and as Maurice watched, she dipped it into the lake.
Immediately the acid in the water
began dissolving it away
in a swift fizz of bubbles.

But Maurice would not change his mind;
he knew that acid did not affect rubber—
and it would make a great scene in their next film!
He floated out on the lake with Gilbert,
the two of them disappearing now and then
behind clouds of fetid steam.
They measured the water's acidity and temperature,
then clipped a sample bottle to a steel cable
and lowered it 696 feet to the bottom of the lake.
As they pulled up the sample,
the clips dissolved and the bottle sank . . .

The next day they found a new bottle
and made new clips from a different material
and paddled out on the acid lake once again.
And this time it worked!
Then a breeze pushed them away from shore
and it took over an hour to return to safety.

Katia was relieved that Maurice
was done floating on the lake, and glad
that the acid burns on his hands
were not serious.

Meanwhile, a mosquito bite on Katia's knee
had become infected and she couldn't walk.
That evening they found a horse
she could ride down the mountain,
with Maurice walking alongside.
Katia was in the hospital
for three weeks—but nearby
another volcano was erupting,
so the rest of the team stayed busy.

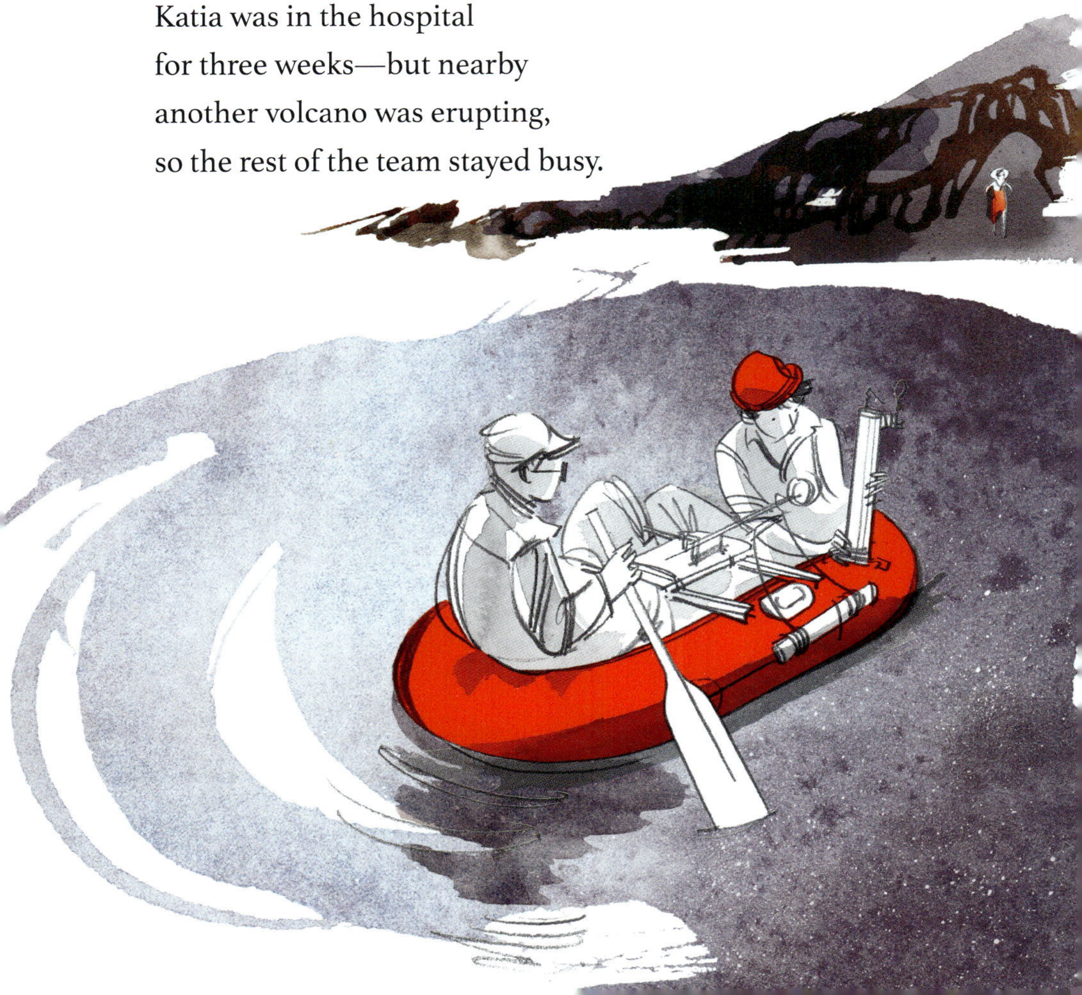

One volcano
they were all looking forward to
was Krakatau. Its eruption
was one of the largest in recorded history
and was similar to that of Santorini:
Over three days in August 1883,
there were four huge explosions.
The largest was so loud
it was heard in Bangkok, Saigon,
Manila, and Perth—and as far
as 3,000 miles away on tiny
Rodrigues Island, near Madagascar.
Towering columns of gas and ash
rose above Krakatau and covered the sea
with rafts of floating pumice.
When the columns collapsed onto the water,
tsunami waves as tall as eleven-story buildings
rushed outward in all directions.
More than 36,000 people died.

Survivor Stories

Krakatau, Dutch East Indies (now Indonesia)

August 1883

Old ships' guide—Anyer, Java

He'd lived all his life in Anyer,
and for many years had guided ships
safely through the Sunda Strait
between the islands of Java and Sumatra.
At first he'd paid no attention to the volcano,
but during the night the explosions
shook his house so much,
he feared it would collapse.
As he walked along the beach
at daybreak, ash and pumice
fell from the sky.
Out in the water was what seemed
like a range of hills, moving toward shore.
He realized it was a high ridge of water—
and it would soon reach the town.
He turned and ran for his life.
A few minutes later he heard the crash
as the wave hit. Everything was engulfed.
Houses were swept away
and trees were thrown down.
He reached some high ground . . .
and that was where the wave caught him.

It lifted him off his feet and carried him inland
until he hit something and clutched at it.
It was a palm tree.
He held on as the water swept by, slowed,
then flowed back toward the sea.
Floating past him were the bodies
of his friends and neighbors.
Only a handful of people survived.
In just a few minutes, the town
where he'd lived all his life
had become a morass of fallen trees,
wrecked homes, and the dead.

Johanna—Ketimbang, Sumatra

As the wife
of the district administrator,
Johanna lived in a house
with a grand view of Krakatau,
only twenty-four miles away. Every day
she watched sailing ships and steamships
pass through the strait to or from Europe.
That day, instead of a view, it was dark
with falling ash. From the balcony
she could see that the sea had gone away
as if the tide was very low—
but it should have been high.
Then a loud roar approached quickly
and a great wave washed away the stairs

and destroyed her husband's office.
He barely escaped by climbing a tree.
They set loose the horses and other animals
and fled with their three children.
The roar of another wave made it seem
as if the sea was trying to catch them.

The only place they could think to go
was their tiny cottage, four hundred feet above sea level.
After walking three hours through darkness
they arrived and found thousands of townspeople
around their home on all sides, crying and praying.
The explosions from the volcano were so loud,
no one could sleep. Early in the morning
they were told the town had disappeared,
swept away by the waves.

That afternoon,
someone burst inside, shouting
"Shut the doors! Shut the doors!"
and suddenly the world was pitch black.
Ash shot upward like fountains
through cracks in the floorboards.
Johanna was thrown to the ground
and didn't realize she had been burned
by an ash flow that had rushed over the sea.
When she tried to clean her arms and hands
she saw her skin was hanging in shreds.

Outside the cottage, a thousand people
died from burns.

Days passed,
and when the air cleared
and the sun finally shone through,
Johanna could see across the water,
now gray with floating pumice.
Where was Krakatau?
It had disappeared.
Along the shore below, the sea
was covered with the roofs of houses,
fallen trees, and dark shapes
that only later she learned
were corpses.

The Child of Krakatau

Indonesia

May–December 1971

When the 1883 eruptions were over,
only a tiny part of Krakatau remained.
But later, where it used to be,
a new volcanic island was born;
it was named Anak Krakatau—
"the Child of Krakatau."

It took five hours for the Vulcan Team
to reach Anak Krakatau by fishing boat.
They unloaded their supplies
and waved goodbye to the crew,
who promised to return in three days.
They were the only people
on the entire island.

Everything was black—
the cinders on the ground
and the sand on the beach.
Only steam and gas rose from the mountain,
but evidence of past eruptions
was everywhere.
Blocks of lava of all sizes
had been blasted out of the vent

and now lay in the craters they made
when they'd fallen from the sky.

The team climbed to the summit,
put on their protective masks,
and collected gas samples
from the orange and yellow fumaroles.

The island had no shade, no vegetation,
and no breeze. The black cinders
baked all day under the hot equatorial sun
and radiated steady heat at night.
The team used up their water supplies quickly
and then collected dew from the tents each morning—
but it wasn't enough for six people.
They even drank the special distilled water
that was needed for sampling gases.
It was so stifling that no one felt like exploring
or making measurements.
All they could do was wait
for the boat to return.

And when it finally did,
the fishermen offered them
freshly caught fish, coconuts,
and all the water they could drink.

Over the seven months
of the Indonesia expedition
the team traveled by dirt roads,
crowded city streets, boats, ships, and ferries
to visit volcanoes on six different islands.
At each volcano they measured temperatures,
collected samples of rock, water, and gas,
and noted hazards to the people
who lived nearby.

And somehow Katia and Maurice
also found time to finish writing their first book,
about volcanoes and earthquakes.

The Town That Fought a Volcano

Heimaey, Iceland

January 1973

Halfway through a quiet breakfast on a Tuesday,
in the house they shared with Katia's parents,
Katia and Maurice heard the radio announce
an eruption off the coast of Iceland.
One day later, on the deck of a fishing trawler
approaching the little island of Heimaey,
they watched as a column of steam and ash
rose into the sky.

Within a few hours of the start of the eruption,
in the middle of the cold winter night,
the boats of the town's fishing fleet
had evacuated nearly the entire island—
five thousand people. The boats were in the harbor
only because a storm the previous day
had prevented the fleet from fishing.

Now the boats were back, filling up
with the last few people leaving their homes
and the first loads of rescued belongings.
Maurice and Katia helped them move beds,
TVs, refrigerators, and other valuables.

Away from the harbor, the town was under attack.
Molten lava shot into the sky, and lava cinders
fell like black hail. Dusty ash drifted through the air.
Closer to the new cinder cone, larger lava blobs
fell like hot bombs. One had smashed the church roof
and burned everything inside. The noise from the vent
was like a sputtering jet engine; even standing side by side,
Katia and Maurice couldn't hear each other talk.

They found a hotel, and the owner let them have
any room they wanted. There were no other guests,
and he was certain the eruption
would destroy the building. They chose a room
with a view of the fountaining lava.
Explosions from the vent
and the clatter of cinders on the metal roof
woke them again and again during the night.

By the second morning the cinders had piled so high
Maurice and Katia couldn't use the hotel's front door—
they had to climb out the second-floor windows.
During the four days they were on the island
the cinder cone grew 344 feet in height, and they saw
houses buried by cinders, burned by lava bombs,
or knocked down by lava flows. They took photos
and filmed everything they could—
including the determination of the residents
to save as much of their town as possible.

When Maurice and Katia returned home,
they talked about Heimaey on French radio and TV.
When they showed their films, they collected money
to help the residents of Heimaey rebuild their homes . . .
whenever the eruption might end.

Survivor Stories

Heimaey, Iceland

1973

Gunnar

He had evacuated the island
with everyone else,
but three days later he returned
to help save valuables
in homes close to the eruption.
Everything in the abandoned houses
was packed up and carried out.
The lava flow creeped slowly,
but when it pushed in
through the windows
they had to give up
and retreat.

Magnús

When the ash and cinders
first started falling
there was only a little, but soon
it was like a thick black snowstorm
that drifted over everything.

Heavy chunks of glowing lava
the size of tennis balls

broke skylights and windows
and set fire to what was inside.
Magnús nailed boards over the openings
so it wouldn't happen again.

When other volunteers came to the island,
he helped as they went from house to house
nailing sheets of corrugated metal
over all the windows facing the volcano.
And then they used heavy beams
to prop up ceilings
and shoveled roofs clean
so the houses wouldn't collapse
under the weight of the cinders.

As the eruption went on
the magma began emitting carbon dioxide,
an invisible, deadly gas.
Carbon dioxide is heavier than air,
and it filled basements
and low areas on the ground.
Magnús lost count
of all the dead cats he saw.

Friðrik

As keeper of the aquarium,
Friðrik also paid close attention
to how the birds on the island

were affected by the eruption.
In the center of town
he kept finding seagulls,
grebes, and snow buntings
that had flown down
and landed in a layer of gas.
Without enough oxygen
they had died.

Gunnar

When he began saving things
from his own apartment,
Gunnar had trouble.
The toxic gas from the volcano
had filled the rooms,
and its sulfur smell
flowed toward him
when he opened the front door.
He had to take deep breaths
of the cold outside air
and then not breathe at all
as he rushed inside
to grab things
and carry them out
one by one.

Magnús

When he worked with a team
helping save valuables
from the larger buildings
in the center of town,
they all lit candles.
If the candles went out,
there was not enough oxygen
to breathe.
To go down
into the basements
was impossible
unless they wore
gas masks.

After two months
the lava flow changed its path
and pushed into the town. House
after house was broken, burned,
knocked down, and covered over
by the thick black lava.
Near the harbor, the flow
reached the power station
and could not be stopped.
The concrete building crumbled.
As every light on Heimaey went out,
some of the men watching
began to weep.

Friðrik

Without electricity,
the aquarium's fish tanks
could not function.
But right next door
was the fire station,
and as soon as the firemen
started up their generator
they connected it
to the aquarium
to keep the fish
alive.

Magnús

With the streets dark
and the houses dark,
the town felt abandoned.
Over the next days
so many places from his childhood
disappeared under the lava.
Magnús was sure everything
would be lost.

The Town That Fought Lava with Water

Heimaey, Iceland

April 1973

Two months after the start of the eruption,
Maurice and Katia heard that something interesting
was happening on Heimaey. So for a few days
they visited again, and brought along
team members Roland and Michel.

The vent was quieter than in January
and was no longer burying the town
in ash and cinders. But the lava flow
was covering more and more of the island—
and the team saw what the islanders were doing
to save the town and their way of life.

When the lava had reached the waterfront,
the island faced a serious new threat.
If lava shut off the harbor from the sea,
the fishing fleet would have no home—
and without the fleet, no one
on the island could make a living.
So forty-three big pumps were brought in
to cool the lava by spraying it with seawater

twenty-four hours a day
for weeks
and weeks
and weeks.

Bulldozers and a crane helped place pipes
over the surface of the hot lava
to direct water to the right areas.
But most of the work moving pipes
was done by people wearing heavy boots
to insulate them from the heat
as they moved through clouds of steam
while the lava flow shifted and creaked
under their feet.

The pumps ran continuously for 103 days,
helping to slow down the lava flow
and slightly change its direction
before the eruption finally stopped.
The harbor was saved!

Even with all the dangerous work
done to save the town
over the five-month-long eruption,
only one person died—
he was suffocated in a basement
by poisonous gas.

Heimaey's new volcano was named Eldfell ("Fire Mountain"), and its eruption ended on July 3, 1973. The ash and cinders that covered the town were removed from streets and yards. The thick lava flow that had destroyed so many buildings was still hot, so water pipes were installed and for more than ten years they provided heat for nearly all the buildings on the island. Along walking paths on the lava flow are signs that show where streets used to be, and "gravestones" marking destroyed houses. Each gravestone lists the name of the house, the year it was built, the day it was destroyed by the eruption, and the thickness of the lava rock now covering it. The ruins of a house that was buried for forty years under ash and cinders is now preserved in the Eldheimar museum. Visitors can learn the story of the family who lived there and see what they had to leave behind during the evacuation. And each year in early July a celebration called Goslokahátíð commemorates the day the eruption finally ended.

Going on Tour

France

1973

Maurice and Katia's lives would soon change.
A company representing French explorers
offered to send them on tour all over the world
to show their films of volcanoes
to audiences interested in travel, nature,
history, and other cultures.

But first, they needed to create a ninety-minute movie.

So they combined their footage from Heimaey
with footage they already had from Stromboli, Etna,
and other volcanoes in Italy; the ruins of Pompeii;
Santorini in Greece; and the extinct craters
in central France.

Their first full-length movie showcased
the exciting history of the volcanoes of Europe.

The images they chose were beautiful
and powerful and thrilling: volcanic activity
that most people—even other volcanologists—
might never see in person.

In many scenes, Katia and Maurice
seemed dangerously close to lava fountains
and explosions and falling rocks—
but most scenes weren't quite as risky
as they appeared.

Each time they showed their movie,
they stood off to the side and narrated,
explaining to the audience about lava and cinders
and different kinds of eruptions,

and telling stories about their expeditions—
what went right, what went wrong,
and whatever mistakes they'd made
that they could joke about.

The audiences loved the film
and how Maurice and Katia told their stories.
And Maurice, especially,
loved having an audience.

With a packed tour schedule,
Maurice and Katia soon decided
they should not present their movie together.

If Katia toured the movie in West Africa
or Maurice toured it in France or Germany,
the other one would be at home
and ready to leave at a moment's notice
whenever a volcano erupted—
anywhere.

The money they earned from touring
allowed Maurice and Katia
to keep visiting volcanoes
and continue creating movies
to share with the world.

The Exploration Prize

Paris, France

February 1975

For their expeditions
to volcanoes all over the globe,
Katia, Maurice, and Roland were summoned
to the Elysée Palace to receive
the Louis Liotard Prize for Exploration.

After all the difficulties they'd weathered
in Iceland, after Katia's hospital stay
in Indonesia, after the dangers they'd faced
on almost too many volcanoes to count,
Katia felt a sudden panic when the door opened
and the president of France walked in.

But he greeted them warmly,
asked questions, and put them at ease
before presenting them
with the symbol of the prize,
the Statue of Knowledge—
a human figure freeing itself
from the confines
of solid rock.

Failure!
Ol Doinyo Lengai, Tanzania

January 1977

The East African Rift,
where Africa is slowly splitting apart,
is studded with volcanoes. Huge,
medium, or small ones; extinct,
active—or even dormant,
like Tanzania's Mount Kilimanjaro,
one of the largest volcanoes on Earth.
Would it ever erupt again?
As with all dormant volcanoes,
the answer was
Maybe.

It took days for Maurice and Katia
and their friend André
to climb to the top, led by two guides
who were born in villages at its base
and knew the mountain well.

Would the guides also lead them
up Ol Doinyo Lengai? *Yes*.

Ol Doinyo Lengai
is the only volcano in the world

that erupts a strange lava
called natrocarbonatite,
which has so much sodium and calcium
its composition is like limestone.
But what did its molten lava look like?
How hot was it? How did it behave?

No one knew.

Maurice and Katia
hoped to be the very first
to find out.

But which set of dirt roads
would get them from Kilimanjaro
to Ol Doinyo Lengai?
Different people gave different answers.
Eventually they found the way,
but storm clouds were filling the sky.

They knew they were near,
but they couldn't yet see the volcano.
What they did see was a great cloud of dust
coming closer and closer . . .
and then the truck began to shake.

Suddenly they were surrounded
by animals: giraffes and buffaloes,

zebras and wildebeests,
warthogs, hyenas, and jackals
kicking up dust in a stampede
to escape the lightning storm.

Once the animals had passed
and the shaking stopped
and the dust settled,
everyone sat in silence.
For just a moment
they had forgotten about volcanoes.

When Maurice started driving again,
from around a bend
the mountain appeared,
pale like a ghost
against the dark, cloudy sky.

They made camp for the night,
and the storm passed them by.
At four in the morning,
with headlamps providing
the only light, they began the
6,000-foot climb to the summit.

On Kilimanjaro, every footstep
had been on good trails
used by many people every day.

But on Ol Doinyo Lengai
there were no trails at all,
and the steep slopes
seemed covered with dry mud.
Their feet sank in and kicked up dust.

After a few hours they stopped to rest
and the guides began talking in Swahili.
"*Hatari*," they said. Danger.
They were far from home, far
from the mountain they knew.
This mountain did not feel safe.
If something happened,
what would their children do
without them?

The guides refused to go farther
and walked away down the slope.
Maurice and Katia followed them.
André continued climbing
until a cliff blocked the way,
and then he turned back too.
They had gotten so close
to something amazing . . .
only to fail.

After the Big Blast

Mount St. Helens, Washington, USA

July 1980

Maurice and Katia had mostly visited
basaltic volcanoes, where molten lava
shoots upward in tall red fountains
and pours downhill in bright red streams.

But there were no lava streams
when Mount St. Helens erupted on May 18, 1980.
Instead, a great landslide
destroyed the top of the mountain,
leaving it 1,300 feet lower than before
and allowing molten rock to explode from inside.
The landslide buried a valley,
and the explosion flattened 230 square miles of forest.
Ice and snow melted to fill rivers with mud,
and ash fell from the sky as far away
as Wisconsin and Oklahoma.

The Kraffts visited two months later.
The explosions had stopped
and a new lava dome
was oozing up into the crater.

They hired a helicopter and pilot
to visit the damaged areas.

When they met Harry,
who knew the area well
and was mapping the deposits
of the huge landslide,
he offered to be their guide.
They flew over what had been forests
but now looked like combed hair—
the huge fir trees stripped of branches
and knocked over, all the tree trunks
pointing away from the mountain.
When the helicopter landed
they could see where the blast
had ripped the bark off the trees
before snapping them like toothpicks.

They flew down the rivers,
following the paths of the mudflows
that swept away houses and bridges,
filled valleys, and clogged
the mighty Columbia River,
making it too shallow for cargo ships.

They looked down on Spirit Lake,
where a tsunami wave from the landslide
had sloshed water 850 feet up the far shore.
The lake was now covered
with thousands of floating dead trees.

After days of flying around the mountain
they had seen everything they'd hoped to see—
except an eruption.
They unloaded their gear from the helicopter,
drove to their motel, and turned on the TV.
The volcano had just erupted! They had missed it!

They rushed back to the airport
and begged a pilot to take them up in a small plane.
The dome in the crater was gone—blasted to bits.
Suddenly another explosion began,
and a new column of ash rose into the sky.
After that eruption weakened and stopped,
a third one sent more ash towering above them
and above all the other planes and helicopters
that were now circling the mountain.
Maurice and Katia filmed and took photos
until the daylight faded and the ash column
glowed pink and purple in the sunset.

This eruption changed the volcano
and changed their plans.
They stayed an extra week,
studying the deposits left by ash flows
that had rushed out of the crater.
The deposits were bright gray,
with blocks of pumice sticking out
of powdery volcanic ash.

When Katia stepped into one, the fresh dust
puffed out under the soles of her boots.
She had to be careful not to sink too deep—
the blocks and ash were still very hot.
How hot? They bought a wooden curtain rod
and pushed it down into the deposit.
The wood caught fire immediately,
and ash shot out from around the hole.

Exactly how these ash flows moved was a mystery,
and Maurice and Katia were fascinated.

Harry Glicken, who guided the Kraffts at Mount St. Helens, had been working for the United States Geological Survey (USGS) when the mountain first began to show activity in March 1980. For two weeks he had been keeping watch from the monitoring site known as Coldwater II about six miles north of the mountain's summit. But Harry needed to fly to California to meet with his university advisor. Beginning the night of May 17, his friend and colleague, David Johnston, agreed to take over at Coldwater II until Harry returned. And so it was David who, at 8:32 the very next morning, was the first to see the north flank of the mountain shiver and begin moving in a huge landslide—and then the explosion that knocked down trees as far as nineteen miles away. Harry had not yet left for California, and when he heard about the eruption he joined three helicopter searches over the blast zone to look for David. No sign of David's body was ever found. Harry was heartbroken and blamed himself for David's death. He spent years mapping the deposits of the landslide to understand how it had moved and why some parts of it crumbled while others remained as huge, hill-sized blocks.

Seeing Volcanoes

La Soufrière, Guadeloupe; Usu and Sakurajima, Japan; Nyiragongo, Democratic Republic of the Congo; Galunggung, Indonesia; El Chichón, Mexico; Aucanquilcha, Chile; Tungurahua and Cotopaxi, Ecuador; Mount Etna, Italy

1981–83

A movie camera
captures motion and sound,
and that was how Maurice
wanted to experience volcanoes—
the sudden *BOOM!* of an explosion,
bright bits of lava arcing high
before falling back to earth,
and red lava rivers
rushing away from the vent.

For Katia, using a still camera
allowed her to capture features
that Maurice's movie camera missed.
In science, the smallest details
might lead to important discoveries—
and in art, sometimes details
are everything.

When she was younger,
Katia had painted pictures,
and as a photographer her artist's eye
found the best composition for an image,
examined the range of textures,
and noticed the gradual change
of one color into another.

In the field, Maurice and Katia
always collected every sample they might need,
and took all the images they could.
It would be too expensive to go back—
besides, an eruption could change or end
at any time, without warning.
They might only have one chance.

At each volcano they worked hard
to get just the right footage and photos
so their films would be beautiful,
interesting, and informative.

They also wanted a few scenes
that would make the audience laugh—
at Maurice and Katia's own mistakes,
like having their pants eaten away
by volcanic gases,
or at silly things
they filmed just for fun,

like Maurice frying eggs
in a skillet
on hot lava.

At Home (Sometimes)

Wattwiller, Alsace, Eastern France

1984

"In one year, I am a writer, a movie maker, a scientist,
and an adventurer and so on—and when you mix
all this, it is fantastic!"
—Maurice

"The volcanoes are our children . . . sometimes very nasty,
spoiled children that demand all of our attention.
We cannot even make plans because we may have to
suddenly go and leave everything.
We have never [had] a quiet life. We can never schedule anything.
We may plan a holiday, but we never go, because
a volcano erupts and we have to go [there instead]."
—Katia

Since 1976, Katia and Maurice
had a house of their own—
but often it didn't seem like it.
Sometimes they returned from one eruption
only long enough to re-pack and fly to another.
And even when they weren't on a volcano,
they might have been traveling across Europe
or around the world to screen their movies
and talk about volcanoes.

Over the years, Maurice and Katia
visited over 300 volcanoes,
saw more than 175 eruptions,
and gave five thousand lectures
to more than four million people.
They showed their movies, they answered questions,
they sold and autographed their books.

Of the 365 days in a year, Katia and Maurice
often spent only about 90 days at home.
But even at home they stayed busy:
Katia selected her best photos
for magazines that wanted to print them.
Maurice edited movie footage for their next film
and replied to letters from other scientists.
They both wrote books. Katia answered mail
from children all over the world.
And like some other volcanologists,
they sent reports and photos of eruptions
to the United States' Smithsonian Institution,
which provided those volcano updates
to scientists all around the world.

The Kraffts' house gradually became more
than just the place where they worked
and ate and slept. It became a shrine
to volcanoes, to the science of volcanology,

and to the many ways volcanoes
are understood and respected or feared
by cultures around the world.

A visitor to their home would have seen
native masks from Bali and Papua New Guinea,
colorful ikat cloth from Sulawesi,
paintings and engravings of volcanoes,
scenes of lava flows painted on a lampshade
and on a stained-glass window,
a two-hundred-pound volcanic bomb
from the Chaîne des Puys,
half-melted forks and bottles
from the city of Saint-Pierre,
and thousands of books
about every aspect of volcanology,
including many that were old and rare.

Although their house was in Wattwiller,
the island of Réunion, in the Indian Ocean,
was like their second home.
The island's volcano, Piton de la Fournaise—
Furnace Peak—became their favorite.
Whenever a new eruption began,
a friend would phone them right away.
After a direct flight from Paris, the Kraffts
could be watching the eruption
the very next day.

"Little by little, we and [Maurice's parents] realized that we had lost them. The volcanoes had stolen them from us."
—Katia's mother

Réunion is a French tropical island in the Indian Ocean east of Madagascar. Like Hawai'i, its basalt volcano is fed by a hot spot that brings hot rock upward from near the Earth's core. Maurice and Katia helped create La Cité du Volcan (Volcano City), an interpretive center that educates the island's inhabitants and visitors about volcanoes around the world, and especially about Réunion's active volcano, Piton de la Fournaise.

A Present, a Photo

Mauna Loa, Hawai'i, USA

March 25, 1984

"My birthday! We were there! It was my most wonderful birthday present! Fantastic!!"
—Maurice

Kīlauea volcano,
on the Big Island of Hawai'i,
had been erupting for a year,
and Katia and Maurice were visiting again.
Suddenly, Kīlauea's bigger neighbor,
Mauna Loa, began erupting too—
on Maurice's birthday!

They hired a helicopter
and flew beyond the rainforest
up toward the barren summit.
Fire fountains of lava fed red rivers
that spilled quickly down the slope,
while campers surprised by the eruption
hurried to escape the danger.

Strapped-in safely but leaning out
the helicopter's open door,
Katia took her most famous photograph:

streams of lava joining together and parting
so that they looked just like the arms and legs
of someone in motion—perhaps Pele,
the goddess of volcanoes
in Hawaiian myths.

Katia titled the photo
Pele Dancing.

Pele, the volcano goddess in the myths of the Hawaiian people, is said to have arrived first on the island of Kaua'i, and created fiery volcanic craters using her magic digging tool. But her older sister, Nāmakaokaha'i, the goddess of the sea, fought with her again and again, forcing Pele to move on to Oahu, Moloka'i, Maui, and then Hawai'i (the Big Island)—an order that matches the ages of volcanism on the islands. She dug a final fire pit, Halema'uma'u crater in the caldera of Kīlauea volcano, where many believe she still resides. According to the myths, Pele is responsible for the eruptions of Kīlauea and Mauna Loa volcanoes, and when she stamps her feet the ground trembles with earthquakes. Even now, fruit, flowers, flower garlands (leis), and alcohol are left at the rim of Halema'uma'u crater as offerings to Pele.

Maurice-and-Katia

Wattwiller, Alsace, Eastern France

1985

"Me, Katia, and the volcanoes; it is a love story."
—Maurice

"We can't imagine living any other way."
—Katia

Some of their friends
said it was hard
to talk just about Maurice
and not Katia, or just about Katia
and not Maurice. It was
Maurice-and-Katia
or Katia-and-Maurice—
together, always.

Still, Maurice and Katia
were very different from each other.
Maurice was tall and strong, with a loud voice
and an even louder laugh.
Katia was delicate and graceful
and easy to smile—but much quieter
than Maurice.

They were both friendly and charming
while staying determined in their goal
of making films and writing books
to educate and inspire people
about volcanoes and volcanology.

When they talked about volcanoes
they were serious—though when the questions
were about Maurice and Katia themselves,
they found ways to be funny.

When asked how many eruptions he had seen,
Maurice said, "You cannot find
another single volcanologist
that has seen so many . . ." and then
Katia kicked him in the leg. "But Katia!
Katia has seen twenty eruptions more than me,
because sometimes I cannot go . . ."

Maurice liked to say, "I am the whale
and Katia is the pilot fish,"
meaning that he was so much larger
than Katia—and also that it was he
who decided where to go
and Katia would follow, like pilot fish
follow larger fish.

And Katia once said,
"We do everything together, Maurice and I.
We can't work without each other.
I like it when he walks in front of me.
Since he is twice my weight, I know
that wherever he goes I can also go.
I follow him because if he's going to die,
I'd rather be with him."

But Katia did not just follow Maurice.
Katia organized every expedition.
She made sure they knew
how to get where they were going,
and had everything they needed
for each trip to succeed.

The Buried City—and the Idea

Nevado del Ruiz, Colombia

November 1985

The news reached France
from the other side of the world:
A volcano in South America had erupted.
The eruption melted ice and snow,
and the meltwater mixed with soil,
and the mud flowed into valleys.
Houses were washed away,
villages disappeared,
and 23,000 people died.

Katia flew to South America—without Maurice,
because he was on tour with their latest movie,
about the marvelous world of volcanoes.

In France, Maurice's gorgeous images
showed the beauty of volcanoes.
In Colombia, Katia saw devastation.

At the edge of a lake of mud
where the city of Armero had been,
Katia fought off packs of hungry dogs,
saw smashed buildings
and bodies half submerged in mud.

Everything smelled like death—
her clothes, her skin, each breath she took.

It was all too much.

Katia called Maurice
on the other side of the world.
Through tears she asked *Why? Why? Why?*
The volcano had been rumbling for a year,
  so why was no one prepared?
The entire city was built on an old mudflow,
  so why did no one realize
  that mudflows would come again?
The Colombian volcanologists
had given a warning,
  so why didn't their government listen?

There were no good answers.

This could happen again somewhere else
unless something changed.
Maurice and Katia realized
they could be the ones to do it:
Their film tours mostly took them to cities
with audiences that might never see a volcano—
but perhaps they could find other ways
to explain the hazards of volcanoes
so the people who lived close to them

would know how to stay safe
when their volcanoes woke up.

Survivor Stories

Nevado del Ruiz, Colombia

November 1985

Slaye

Sixteen-year-old Slaye
saw the ash begin falling
in the late afternoon.
It was like soft sand,
covering the streets, cars,
and roofs of Armero.
When rain began an hour later
she could smell sulfur in the air.
But loudspeakers outside the church
urged everyone to stay calm.

Juan

When ash fell again that night,
Juan and his friends
turned on a radio.
The mayor was talking
and he said not to worry.
So they listened to music
until suddenly the radio
went silent.
Then the lights went out
and there was a noise

like things falling over
and breaking apart.
But there were no alarms,
no sirens. They went outside,
where the only light
was from the headlights of cars
careening through the streets
as people rushed to escape.

Slaye
At 11:15 that night
the mud came
and people began screaming.

María
María rushed outside with her children,
but the mud was faster.
It caught them, pulled them
away from each other,
and carried them
through the darkness,
the children screaming
as they bobbed like corks.
María leaned toward her baby,
stretching as far as she could.
She touched the tiny hand
once,
twice,

and then the mud
took her daughter
away.

Juan
The street
became a churning river
filled with beds, furniture,
and overturned cars.
Then came a wall of mud
studded with boulders,
and even the strong buildings
made of cement
were crushed and broken
into pieces.

Slaye
A neighbor's house collapsed
and Slaye rushed out to the street
with her grandmother, aunt, and uncle.
A friend grabbed Slaye's hand
and the two of them ran
as fast as they could.
When they reached a hill
higher than the mud, they were safe,
but for fifteen long minutes
they listened to the grindings
and splinterings

as the rest of Armero
disappeared.

In the morning
the friends saw that the city
had become a sea of mud.
They spent three days on the hill
without food or water,
hearing the cries of people
trapped and half buried.
When the mud was hard enough
to walk across, they escaped
and Slaye found her grandfather
and one uncle still alive.
She washed mud
from the faces of twenty-nine bodies
but found no one else
from her family,
either living
or dead.

Meeting with an Ash Flow

Mount Augustine, Alaska, USA

August 1986

Maurice and Katia
had been to many kinds of eruptions,
but they had not yet filmed
all the types of volcanic hazards.
So when their friend Jürgen called from Alaska
to tell them a lava dome was spilling out
of the crater of Mount Augustine,
they knew they had to join him.

They arrived from France two days later
and helicoptered to the volcano's little island.
A layer of low cloud hid the summit,
but over and over again, a dusty ash flow
appeared suddenly through the clouds,
moving at ninety miles per hour
down the volcano's steep slope.

Though they couldn't see it happening,
they knew that each ash flow
began when lava rocks hotter than flames
spilled out of the crater and broke apart
into smaller and smaller pieces,

swelling up into a searing mass
of dust and gas.

The helicopter landed
in what seemed like a good spot,
but Maurice wanted a better view.
The pilot took them closer,
then he and Jürgen
moved the helicopter
to where it seemed safer.

But when Jürgen saw the Kraffts
struggle to move their equipment
into the best position, he and the pilot
climbed up to help.

They set up their cameras
only 150 feet away from the path
of the flows. Maurice filmed;
Katia and Jürgen took photographs;
the helicopter pilot watched, entranced.

The ash flows came one after another,
every twenty minutes—in eerie silence.
As each one passed, their hairs stood up
from its static electricity.

Suddenly the next flow was bigger
and went farther down the mountain.
When it slowed to a stop,
the breeze cooled the dusty ash
and blew it in their direction,
enveloping them in a thick, gritty fog.

They couldn't see anything,
and the air smelled of sulfur.
"*Ça suffit!*" said Maurice. That's enough!
They gathered their equipment and left.

So many things about ash flows
were still unknown. No one
had filmed the flows from so close before—
and now the three of them had done it!
But the next day, they all asked themselves
if they'd taken too great a risk.

Katia and Maurice decided the answer was *No*—
because studying the flows up close
was necessary to understand them better.
Someone had to do it.
They could calculate the risk—
and minimize it—
but risk would always be there.

But for Jürgen, who had a family, it was *Yes*—
and the more he thought about it,
the more danger he felt he'd been in.
For years he was so angry,
he refused to even talk
with Maurice and Katia.

The Plan
Hilo, Hawai'i, USA

January 1987

"Volcanoes are the most beautiful thing in nature, but they kill.
But it is one of my dreams that volcanoes no longer kill."
—Maurice

"Technical reports don't mean a thing to people who
don't know about volcanoes. So we thought we'd make
film programs instead. If we show a government images of
the victims, the damage, the dangers, they might believe us,
we might convince them."
—Katia

The Hawaiian Volcano Observatory
was founded in 1912 with the motto
"No more burned or buried cities."
For its seventy-fifth anniversary celebration,
Maurice and Katia created a film
about the observatory
and about the history of volcanology.

The film included images
from Katia's visit to Colombia:
dead bodies and the rubble of buildings
after the mudflows
buried the city of Armero.

More than four hundred volcanologists
from all over the world saw the film,
and some of them realized the same thing
that Katia and Maurice had:
If the people of Armero
could have seen images like those,
they would have understood what to expect
when their volcano erupted.
Many more people would have survived.

Those scientists wanted to help Katia and Maurice
with their idea for a film about volcanic hazards,
so it could be shown to anyone near a volcano
anywhere in the world.

Maurice offered to choose the right film footage
and provide it for free. Others could
assemble the footage into a video
and translate it into multiple languages.

The Burned City

Mount Pelée, Martinique

March 1988

The city of Saint-Pierre,
on the island of Martinique,
had once been called "the Paris
of the Caribbean." But in 1902,
during an eruption of Mount Pelée,
an ash flow rushed down the mountain
and surged into Saint-Pierre.
It flattened buildings,
burned the entire city,
sank ships in the harbor,
and killed 29,000 people
in less than ten minutes.

Now Maurice and Katia
were on Martinique for a conference
about explosive volcanism.
With the other volcanologists
gathered around,
Katia pointed out a ridge,
high up on the volcano,
just below the summit.

With a twinkle in her eye
and excitement in her voice,
Katia told how Frank Perret,
an American volcanologist,
had arrived after new eruptions
began in 1929. On that ridge
he built a wooden shack
and watched as ash flows
came down from the lava dome
at the summit. The flows
moved past him on both sides,
because the top end of the ridge
was like the bow of a ship
splitting oncoming waves.

But one day
a much larger flow came,
and he knew there was no time
to run to safety.
He closed the windows
and doors, but the hot dust
swirled in through every crack,
and the gases dried his throat
and left him feeling weak.
After thirty minutes
a breeze cleared the air

and he lit a lantern
to tell his friends in the city
he didn't need to be
rescued.

Perret's notes and photographs
were the first to reveal
how these ash flows formed
and what they looked like
as they moved. But the Kraffts
had done better. They had something
Perret did not—a movie camera.
Their film from Mount Augustine,
shot at twenty-four frames per second,
showed not only *how* the flows changed,
but *how quickly* they could change
as they rushed down the slope,
unstoppable.

Survivor Stories

Mount Pelée, Martinique

May 8, 1902

Ludger

He had been fighting again
and the police were fed up with it.
So they arrested Ludger and put him,
alone, into a special jail cell
with thick stone walls.
Instead of windows, there was only
a metal door with a narrow slit for air.
The door faced out to sea, away
from the mountain.
He spent the night there.

While he waited for breakfast
the next morning,
a cloud of dust suddenly blew in.
It was so hot it burned Ludger's
hands, arms, legs, and back.
He tried using his clothes
to plug up the door slit,
and somehow managed
to not breathe the air
that would have burned his lungs.
The heat faded quickly

but the pain of his deep burns did not.
He had to wait three days
in the locked cell
before being rescued.

Later, Ludger toured America
as part of "The Barnum & Bailey
Greatest Show on Earth."
He was billed as "the man
who lived through Doomsday"
and could be seen in a recreation
of his Saint-Pierre jail cell,
telling the story of the eruption
and his survival in the ruined city.

Havivra

When ten-year-old Havivra
saw the eruption begin,
she ran to her brother's boat
and rowed toward a small cave
where she used to play pirates
with her friends. Ash
and pumice stones burned her,
but she got to the cave.

Almost right away she heard
a great hissing noise
as the ash flow reached the shore,

kicked up a tsunami wave,
and set the sea to boiling.
The wave reached her
and shoved the boat
toward the roof of the cave—
and that's the last thing
she remembered.

Several days later,
rescuers from the French navy
found her unconscious
in the charred boat, adrift,
two miles out at sea.

Of the tens of thousands
who'd been in the city
of Saint-Pierre,
only Havivra, Ludger,
and one other person
survived.

The Strangest Lava

Ol Doinyo Lengai, Tanzania

June 1988

Eleven years
after they had first tried
to climb Ol Doinyo Lengai
and had to turn back,
Maurice and Katia tried again—
this time with scientist friends Jörg,
Celia, Christof, and André.
Two experienced guides led them,
and ten local porters helped carry food
and water and equipment.
After a nine-hour climb
they finally reached the summit—
and it was like stepping
onto another planet.

Down in the gray crater,
a black lake bubbled and burped,
splattering mud into the air
and overflowing onto the ground.
But it wasn't mud. It was lava—
the most fluid molten lava on Earth.
It flowed as a thin black slurry,
but after it hardened it slowly turned gray

and then white, before crumbling
into dust.

Maurice grabbed the thermometer
and became the first person ever
to measure the temperature of this strange lava—
1,004 degrees Fahrenheit.
It was even less hot than they expected:
just half as hot as basalt lava.

And because its temperature was so low,
the weak, reddish glow of the bubbling lava
could only be seen when the sky grew dark.
It was as dim as embers of a campfire
almost burned out.

The group camped in the crater for a week.
They photographed and filmed,
measured temperatures, and sampled gases.
They leaped across the tiny lava flows
and scooped up samples
with a cooking spoon.

But even the least-hot lava in the world
was still hot enough
to blister Maurice's hands
as he worked with the movie camera
close to the ground.

By the last day on the mountain,
Maurice and Katia had used up
all their movie and camera film;
they wandered around the crater
watching the others taking photos
they wished *they* could take.

As soon as they returned home to France,
the Kraffts created a short film
about what they'd seen on Ol Doinyo Lengai.
That film was only ten minutes long—
but when they took it to a conference in Japan
it amazed dozens of volcano experts.
None of them had ever imagined
that natrocarbonatite lava
could behave so differently
from the normal lavas
they all had studied
for years.

The Hazards Video

Wattwiller, Alsace, Eastern France

1989–91

The film project
about volcanic hazards
was moving too slowly
because so many groups
were trying to work together.

Maurice and Katia became impatient.

They began making
a rough version of the video
and completed it in early 1991.
The video described
volcanic tsunamis
  like those from Krakatau,
ash falls, lava flows,
and volcanic gases
  like on Heimaey,
volcanic landslides
  like at Mount St. Helens,
ash flows like those
  from Mount Augustine
  and Mount Pelée,

and volcanic mudflows
like those in Armero.

The Kraffts sent their rough video
to the U.S. Volcano Disaster
Assistance Program,
which was created in 1986
in response to the Armero tragedy.
Copies of the video were then given
to volcano observatories
all around the world.

Expert support is offered by the U.S. Volcano Disaster Assistance Program (VDAP) when a volcano in another country begins waking up. That country can invite VDAP scientists to come and work with them to provide advice and special equipment to monitor the volcano, identify danger zones, and help the local volcanologists figure out if the new activity might just go away—or if it could become more dangerous.

A Sudden Change of Plans

Mount Pelée, Martinique

late May 1991

Maurice and Katia returned to Martinique
three years after their previous visit.
They had been invited as guests of honor
to inaugurate a new museum
about Mount Pelée and the 1902 eruption
that destroyed the city of Saint-Pierre.

There were speeches
by the museum's director,
and the mayor, and the Kraffts.
There was the ribbon-cutting
that officially opened the museum.
There was small talk with everyone
who came for the festivities.

Later, they got a phone call from Japan.
It was their friend Harry, who had studied
the huge Mount St. Helens landslide.
He was now helping map ancient landslides
at Japanese volcanoes. He said
that if they came now, they could watch
ash flows on Mount Unzen.
Maurice had good movie footage

of the ash flows at Mount Augustine,
in Alaska—but what if they could get
even better footage? What if it
could reveal something new?

It was an opportunity
they couldn't pass up.
So they cut their trip short
and flew home to France just long enough
to gather the gear they needed.

They were on a plane to Tokyo
the very next day.

The Day Before

Mount Unzen, Japan

June 2, 1991

When Maurice, Katia, and Harry
arrived at Unzen, the weather was terrible!
There was so much fog and rain
that airplanes and helicopters
were grounded—but that didn't matter,
because even if the sky cleared,
all the aircraft had been reserved
for the news photographers.
The Kraffts would not be able
to get a sense of the area from the air
before deciding where to watch
from the ground.

The only way to see the volcano
was to drive into the evacuated area,
to a hillside overlooking a valley
with a good view of the summit.
The sides of the road
were lined bumper to bumper
with cars and taxicabs.
Radio and TV news reporters
stared up at the mountain,

and photographers set up cameras
with huge telephoto lenses.

At Augustine, they had watched ash flows
rush past in the distance. Here at Unzen,
the flows came straight toward them—
and then turned safely away down the valley,
into the damaged outskirts of the city.

While everyone waited
for the weather to improve,
the Japanese reporters
interviewed Maurice and Katia
about volcanoes
and about Unzen
and about whether they were afraid
to be so close.

"To me, the danger is not important,"
Katia told them. "I am afraid
when I go in the car. But on volcanoes,
I forget everything."

"I am never afraid," Maurice said, grinning,
"because I have seen so many eruptions
in twenty-three years that,
even if I die tomorrow,
I do not care."

That night, Katia and Maurice
discussed when to fly to the Philippines,
where Mount Pinatubo was waking up,
five hundred years after its last eruption.
Katia wanted to go right away.
But Maurice needed another day at Unzen.
He was sure the weather would improve
and he could get the footage he wanted.

The Last Day

Mount Unzen, Japan

June 3, 1991, 4:08 p.m.

As the brown ash flow
moved down the mountain,
swelling up, hiding the volcano,
and blotting out the sky,
it came closer and closer
to where they stood.

Compared to the flows
from earlier that day,
this one had grown much larger.
So large, they knew
that only some of it
would turn safely away.

So large, they surely knew
they could not escape it.

In the short time
before the flow reached them,
did Katia and Maurice look back
over the events in their lives
that had brought them
to this moment
on Unzen?

Or did they study the ash flow
for anything new they could learn,
watching its dark, dusty churning,
its front edge seeming to leap
and leap again, getting closer
and closer—until it was so close
they knew they would not live
to tell its secrets?

The ash flow of June 3, 1991, completely destroyed 49 houses and 130 other buildings. In addition to the Kraffts, it killed forty-one other people and injured nine. They were reporters, photographers, taxi drivers, policemen, and the firefighters and their families who were stationed nearby. Several people were able to escape by driving quickly away from the mountain. Others were just far enough away that they were badly burned but survived. Harry Glicken was nearby but not with the Kraffts when the ash flow formed; he tried to escape but died like his friends Katia and Maurice.

The Warning That Worked

Mount Pinatubo, Philippines

June 15, 1991

Twelve days later,
1,300 miles south of Mount Unzen,
Mount Pinatubo erupted while a strong typhoon
drenched the area with rain.

The eruption column rose twenty-two miles into the sky.
Volcanic ash mixed with the rain
and then fell like wet gray snow,
damaging airplanes and collapsing roofs.
Hot ash flows burned forests and filled valleys.
Mudflows swept down rivers, flooding fields
and washing away houses and bridges.

The huge eruption may have directly affected
more people than any other eruption, ever.
But the volcano itself killed only about 400 people
because 250,000 villagers had been evacuated
from near the mountain, including 60,000
whose homes were completely destroyed.
They moved to safety because so many people—
from the president of the Philippines
    to governors

to village elders
to regular citizens with televisions—
knew what could happen
when Pinatubo erupted . . .

And they knew
because they had learned about ash falls,
ash flows, and mudflows by watching
the video that Maurice and Katia Krafft
had finished just months before.
The video the Kraffts created
for exactly that reason—
in the profound hope
that huge tragedies
like those of Armero
and Saint-Pierre
and Krakatau
and Pompeii
might never
happen
again.

Photos

For her pioneering work on the portable gas analyzer, Katia received the Vocation Prize, presented by the prime minister of France, Jacques Chaban-Delmas, in Paris on December 8, 1969. © MAURICE & KATIA KRAFFT/DUMONT.

Katia using the portable gas analyzer to study fumaroles on the rim of the great crater on Vulcano, in Italy's Aeolian Islands, in July 1970. © MAURICE & KATIA KRAFFT/DUMONT.

The inner walls of the Greek island of Santorini drop steeply from the town of Firá, on the east rim of the caldera. The great Minoan eruption 3,600 years ago was the most recent major eruption. Credit: Lee Siebert, Smithsonian Institution.

No photographs of the climactic eruption of Krakatau in the Dutch East Indies (now Indonesia) on August 27, 1883, have survived, but a photograph from the beginning of the activity three months earlier—on May 27, 1883—was used to make this hand-colored lithograph print. Image: Public domain.

A column of ash and cinders rises above lava fountains from the 1973 eruption on the island of Heimaey, Iceland. On the right is an older cinder cone that formed during an eruption 5,900 years ago. In the foreground is the harbor used by the fishing fleet. Credit: Tom Simkin, Smithsonian Institution.

Maurice and Katia filming the fire fountain of the Eldfell eruption on Heimaey, Iceland, during their follow-up visit in April 1973. When they visited in January, just after the eruption began, the fire fountain was much higher and they could not get this close. © MAURICE & KATIA KRAFFT/DUMONT.

One of Katia's photos, *Pele Dancing,* taken from a helicopter, showing intertwined lava flows during the eruption of Mauna Loa, Hawai'i, USA, on March 25, 1984—Maurice's birthday. © MAURICE & KATIA KRAFFT/DUMONT.

Maurice filming about 150 feet away from an ash flow at Mount Augustine, Alaska, USA. These ash flows were generated by the edge of a growing lava dome spilling out of the crater at the top of the volcano, much like the ash flows at Mount Unzen in Japan. © MAURICE & KATIA KRAFFT/DUMONT.

Postcards showing the city and harbor of Saint-Pierre, Martinique. Left: A hand-tinted image from before the May 8, 1902, eruption of Mount Pelée. Right: The ruins of the city afterward. Photo: Public domain.

The hills in the foreground are the remnants of a huge, ancient landslide from northern California's Mount Shasta volcano (in the background), very similar to the one at Mount St. Helens in 1980, which Harry Glicken studied. Because continued eruptions covered all evidence of the landslide on Mount Shasta itself, it was recognized as a landslide only after the Mount St. Helens eruption. Huge landslides have occurred at many other volcanoes around the world, including in Japan, where Harry was helping to map and understand them in 1991.
Credit: Harry Glicken, U.S. Geological Survey.

Ash flows spread far from the summit of Mount Pinatubo in the Philippines during its climactic eruption on June 15, 1991. © Alberto Garcia/REDUX.

A pair of Maurice and Katia's red knit caps and Maurice's wristwatch, displayed at the Vulcania theme park in the Auvergne region of France. They were not wearing these hats at Mount Unzen on June 3, 1991, but Maurice was wearing this watch. © Claude Grandpey.

Author's Note

Some volcanologists do their research on active volcanoes. They hope to learn how to predict when and where an eruption might start, what kind of hazards it will create and who they will affect, and how to apply knowledge about eruptions at one volcano to help understand the behavior of other volcanoes.

But there are important things to learn from extinct and dormant volcanoes, too. The rocks that a volcano erupted early in its history may be completely hidden beneath all the lava flows and ash layers that erupted later. Over time, erosion by streams can cut into the volcano and allow those early rocks to be studied and sampled.

I did my first volcanology fieldwork in Arizona, California, and Oregon, investigating how pumice layers were formed in small lava domes, and what hazards they might cause. That type of dome doesn't erupt often, and at that time no scientist had ever seen one when it was active. Only by carefully studying features on the domes could I figure out what had happened as the lava squeezed up out of the vent and slowly spread over the ground. The answer was that sudden steam explosions blasted out deep craters, and blobs of dark pumice rose slowly and broke through the surface of the lava flow like the domed shell of a swimming turtle coming up for air . . .

I worked on lava flows in Idaho that were similar to those domes, but millions of years older—and a hundred times larger. Some other volcanologists thought they were much too large to possibly be lava flows, but my research showed why that was not true.

For parts of both studies I used a computer program I wrote to discover how quickly lava flows cool on Earth—and on other planets with different temperatures and atmospheres. One of the things I learned was that on Earth the bubbly pumice at the top of the flow insulates the rest of the lava, so most flows cool very, very slowly!

My research also involved a lot of walking around to map the shapes and features of the lava flows; collecting rock samples and analyzing their textures, compositions, and minerals; and working with tiny crystals to learn about the gases the magma contained before it erupted.

I was halfway through my research project when Mount Unzen began erupting. Volcanologists around the world heard about it through email lists and reports from the Smithsonian Institution's Global Volcanism Network. And then we soon heard the sad news that Katia and Maurice Krafft, Harry Glicken, and too many others had died when a large ash flow swept over them as they observed the volcano. Ten days later, the world was watching Mount Pinatubo in the Philippines. As its activity intensified, a local Phoenix, Arizona, news station wanted to interview a volcanologist, so I ended up on TV for a few minutes talking about what might happen as the eruption continued.

Katia and Maurice Krafft had shown one of their films at a volcanology conference I attended in Santa Fe, New Mexico, but I did not have a chance to meet them. They loved educating people around the world about volcanic activity, and they did it well. But until I began working on *Chasing Eruptions* in 2018, I knew only a small part of their story. I'm especially grateful for the hazards video they were inspired to create, and how, just months after they finished it, that video saved the lives of tens of thousands of people. I wish they had been able to know that.

Curtis Manley

Obsidian Dome, a 550-year-old rhyolite lava dome near Mono Lake in eastern California, USA. Most of the surface of the dome is made up of tan and gray pumice, with smaller amounts of black pumice and obsidian. The highest point shows the location of the vent, from which the lava erupted and spread outward in all directions. © Curtis Manley.

Rock Mesa, a 2,000-year-old rhyodacite lava dome at South Sister volcano near Bend, Oregon, USA. The areas of dark pumice rose to the surface from inside the flow. For scale, the largest explosion crater measures 250 feet across. © Curtis Manley.

Volcanic Hazards from the Kraffts' Video

"By understanding the effects of volcanic eruptions, we can take steps to avoid their deadly consequences. Remembering recent volcanic disasters is a first step for preventing future volcanic tragedies."

Ash falls happen when an exploding volcano blasts molten rock and ash into the air with tremendous force. The largest fragments fall close to the volcano, pebble-sized cinders or pumice can fall a bit farther away, but the dust-sized ash fragments rise into the air, forming a huge, billowing cloud of ash. Once in the air, particles of ash drift with the wind.

If enough material falls on a house or building, the extra weight can form holes in the roof or cause it to collapse entirely, injuring or killing people inside.

Falling ash can strip leaves and limbs from trees. A thick layer of ash can destroy crops and leave farmland unworkable for weeks or months. Fields can be made useless for grazing animals, and water may be unsuitable for drinking.

Falling ash affects people farther from an erupting volcano more than any other type of volcanic activity.

Ash flows are avalanches of hot ash, pumice, and gas that move at high speeds down the slope of a volcano. Ash flows are the most destructive

type of volcanic activity. They are extremely hot and can move across the ground as fast as one hundred miles per hour. Ash flows can knock down and burn everything in their path. You can't outrun an ash flow. As it moves down the side of a volcano, it usually pours into canyons and river valleys. But at the bottom of the volcano, it can spread out across the land into populated areas.

Volcanic mudflows, also called lahars, are floods of water, mud, sand, and rock that rush down river valleys. They turn rivers into torrents of debris moving at up to thirty miles per hour. Mudflows look like

fast-moving rivers of wet concrete. They can uproot and destroy everything in their paths.

Lava flows are formed by molten rock that erupts in fountains or pours across the ground from a vent. Lava can erupt from several vents at one time, the flows merging together to form a fast-moving river of lava. On steep ground, these rivers can flow as fast as twenty miles per hour. On flatter ground, lava flows spread out into broad sheets and usually move less than half a mile per hour. Most lava flows move slowly enough for people and animals to reach safety—but everything else in the way of a lava flow is either burned or covered by molten rock. Farmland covered by lava cannot be used again for many years.

Volcanic landslides happen because volcanoes are weakly constructed of many separate layers of lava, ash, and soil. Huge chunks of a volcano can break away suddenly and without warning. In 1980, Mount St. Helens generated the largest volcanic landslide in recorded history: One side of the volcano broke loose, sliding into a valley as an avalanche moving faster than one hundred miles per hour. It buried the entire valley with rocks and mud up to six hundred feet thick.

Volcanic tsunamis are giant ocean waves that rush onshore with tremendous force. They may consist of one wave or several waves that follow one right after another. Volcanic tsunamis can be triggered by different types of volcanic activity, including eruptions under water, giant landslides, and ash flows that slam into the ocean.

Volcanic gases are released into the air by every active volcano—both between and during eruptions—from cracks and vents located on or near the volcano. Most of the gas is ordinary water vapor, but other types are more dangerous. Sulfur gases sting the nose and throat, and one type smells like rotten eggs; they can also damage crops and corrode metal. Fluorine gas can contaminate grass and sicken and kill livestock. Carbon dioxide gas can be released from vents on a volcano or from crater lakes. Since it is heavier than air, the odorless carbon dioxide sinks to low areas, taking the place of air and oxygen, killing animals and people.

Ash Flows in More Detail

Ash flows are also known as pyroclastic flows. The term "pyroclastic" comes from Greek words that mean "fire broken." Long ago, when volcanoes were completely mysterious, they were thought to erupt due to fire underground, so everyone assumed that the fragments of lava rock and mineral crystals that volcanoes produced were broken by fire.

An ash flow is a cloud of hot ash, pumice, and gas. Pumice is a lightweight rock that forms when sticky molten lava puffs up with bubbles of steamy water vapor. When the pressure in the bubbles gets too high, the pumice breaks apart into tiny shards of glass: volcanic ash. Because the ash flow cloud is so full of ash and pumice, it is denser than air and wants to sink toward the ground and move down the volcano's slope somewhat like an avalanche of snow.

Ash flows form in several different ways, and they don't all behave the same.

- Ash flows like the ones at Mount Augustine and Mount Unzen are created by hot boulders breaking off a growing lava dome. As the boulders roll and bounce down the mountain's slope, they shatter into ash and bits of pumice. Each time a piece of pumice breaks, more steam escapes from the pumice's bubbles, and that steam puffs up the ash flow and keeps it moving. The large, rolling blocks of pumice at the bottom of the flow may follow a stream or river valley, but the ashy cloud above them can move in a different direction—as happened at Mount Unzen.
- Ash flows can also form during the eruption of a large ash column rising up into the atmosphere, like the eruption that the Kraffts saw from the plane at Mount St. Helens in

July 1980. If any part of the column is denser than air, that part can sink downward—even if the rest of it is pushing high into the sky.

- A volcanic blast can create an ash flow, as happened during the May 18, 1980, eruption of Mount St. Helens. The blast of gas, ash, and pumice stones, moving at hundreds of miles per hour, knocked down the forest as far as nineteen miles from the mountain; burned trees, people, and vehicles; and left a layer of ash over everything that remained.

New Videos About Volcanic Hazards

The Kraffts' idea for their hazard video is being expanded and extended by the VolFilm project (https://vimeo.com/volfilm), which is creating short educational films to help communities located near volcanoes. There are films about each volcanic hazard, films about how each hazard affects people, and films of people sharing their experiences with each hazard. Versions of the films are available in many of the languages spoken where people live close to volcanoes: English, French, Spanish, Italian, Turkish, Japanese, Tagalog, and Indonesian.

Different Lavas, Different Eruptions, Different Volcanoes

Eruptions in Hawai'i are not like Mount St. Helens's violent awakening in 1980, because different types of molten rock behave in very different ways. Most magmas (what we call molten rock that is underground) and lavas (molten rock that has come to the surface) are divided into a range of types that have different compositions, temperatures, and viscosities (how "runny" or "sticky" they are).

Basalt lava, like what the Kraffts saw at Heimaey and in Hawai'i, is rich in iron and magnesium and low in silicon; it is the hottest common lava, and the least viscous (the runniest).

If basalt magma does not erupt right away, it can begin to change as mineral crystals grow. The magma's iron and magnesium decrease, its silicon increases, and it becomes cooler and more viscous (stickier). As it changes, we change what name we give it: basalt, andesite, dacite, rhyodacite, and then rhyolite.

All magmas and lavas have gases dissolved in them (like carbon dioxide in a bottle of soda), and when the pressure is released (like when the soda bottle is opened) the gases make bubbles. In runny basalt lava, little bubbles can join together to make large bubbles that rise and burst in the vent, shooting bright bits of lava into the sky, as Maurice and Katia saw at Stromboli.

Magmas with the most silicon are so viscous that the bubbles can't rise through it but instead cause it to puff up into pumice—or even blow it apart into ash, as at Mount St. Helens and Mount Pinatubo. Some eruptions of viscous lava start with explosions and then change to lava oozing up and spreading out from the vent to make a lava flow or dome, as at Mount Augustine and Mount Unzen.

How the lavas erupt and behave controls whether the volcano they build is shaped like a shield, with gentle slopes from runny lavas (Kīlauea, Mauna Loa), or tall with steeper slopes from thick lava flows, ash, and broken rock (Mount St. Helens, Mount Augustine, Mount Pelée, and Mount Unzen).

How Volcanologists Study Volcanoes Today

Over the past several decades, volcanology has improved quickly and in important ways. Volcanologists today use many tools and techniques, some of which were not available to Maurice and Katia. These tools help them understand how volcanoes work, and how to predict when they are likely to become dangerous to the people who live or work nearby.

Most active volcanoes (and many that are dormant) are monitored by **seismometers** that detect seismic waves from earthquakes caused by movement of magma and gases underground. Almost all eruptions are preceded by one or more kinds of earthquakes, and they can help pinpoint exactly where the eruption might occur.

GPS devices, installed on or near a volcano, use the global positioning system of satellites to reveal if a volcano's shape is changing due to accumulation or draining-away of magma. GPS is the same technology that allows a smartphone to provide driving directions, especially where cell coverage is poor or nonexistent.

Observing satellites actively watch the Earth. Some can use radar to measure the height of a volcano's entire surface to detect changes when magma moves underground or erupts. Other satellites can measure increasing temperatures or see plumes of ash, mudflows, or other signs of volcanic unrest.

The **petrology** of lava samples—their compositions, mineral crystals, temperatures, and gas contents—can indicate where the magma was formed and how deep it was before it erupted. This information can sometimes be combined with seismic data to figure out the locations and shapes of magma chambers beneath a volcano.

Katia's portable gas analyzer was state of the art in 1970, but today volcanic gases are primarily measured by **spectroscopy**—which means that light spectra are used to detect what gas molecules are present and how concentrated they are. Volcanologists can now measure the gases from a distance, or they might set up gas monitors that automatically take a small sample of air every minute, determine the amount of carbon dioxide, sulfur dioxide, and hydrogen sulfide in it, and then transmit that data by cellular signals.

Mapping of a volcano's lava flows, ash layers, and mudflow layers from long ago can give a very good idea of what the volcano might do in the future. That knowledge can then be used to create hazard maps that inform the people who live nearby about what their volcano could do whenever it might again become active.

Drones are used more and more to measure lava temperatures; map lava flows, cracks, and other features; and take samples where it is not safe for humans to go.

In many ways, **smartphones** have become essential tools for volcanologists (and for other scientists). With one device, a volcanologist can take geo-referenced photos to document deposits, events, and environmental conditions; can record spoken notes; can use GPS to show location and create maps; and when a cell signal is available can communicate by voice and text, look up information, and connect to databases and real-time monitoring data.

The **internet** allows access to information, but also the ability to watch volcanic activity via webcams and data streams in real time from anywhere in the world; this allows researchers to easily work together as a team even if they are spread across different continents.

On the volcanoes that are the most active—or that are nearest to large cities—many different features are measured regularly so that any changes are noticed right away. Even the smallest changes might reveal important clues to what the volcano could do next.

When dormant volcanoes awaken decades or centuries after their previous eruptions, there may be no human memory of how the volcano behaved in the past. New methods that combine some of the measurements mentioned above, with knowledge of how magma breaks its way to the surface, are being tested to help forecast the probability of the unrest either quieting away or leading to an eruption—and how soon that eruption might happen.

Observatories and Volcanologists

The science of volcanology made a great leap with the creation of volcano observatories. Somewhat like an astronomical observatory that studies planets and stars, a volcano observatory is dedicated to closely studying one or more volcanoes that present hazards to people living or working nearby. The observatory at Vesuvius, founded in 1841, was the world's first. The eruptions of Mount Pelée and two other volcanoes in 1902 led to the creation of more volcano observatories with the goal of understanding volcanic phenomena, predicting eruptions, and preventing deaths. Today, forty-two countries have at least one observatory monitoring and studying their volcanoes. The United States has 161 active volcanoes; they are monitored by five volcano observatories that cover specific regions: Hawai'i, Alaska, the Cascades, California, and Yellowstone. Each volcano observatory is made up of scientists and technicians, the equipment they use, and the buildings and locations where they work.

In addition to the staff at observatories, many other people study volcanoes. Most are either scientists from other government agencies (such as NASA and NOAA) or faculty, students, and staff at universities around the world.

Some volcanologists spend lots of time outdoors mapping deposits, making measurements, or keeping monitoring devices working. Others spend most of their time in a laboratory working with samples or using computers to study the data collected by monitoring equipment. Still others are responsible for informing the public about volcanic activity and the observatory's work, findings, and warnings.

Every volcanologist hopes to learn something new about one or more aspects of volcanic activity, but each scientist goes about it a bit differently from everyone else. And with volcanoes all over the Earth—and on other planets and moons in our solar system—there are many, many different places and ways to study volcanoes.

If becoming a volcanologist interests you, here are some ways you can prepare yourself:

- Read about the different kinds of volcanoes, how they erupt, and how they are studied.
- Visit any volcanoes you can, but be careful and stay safe.
- Take advanced science courses in high school and improve your critical and analytical thinking. Consider attending a summer science camp.
- Learn as much math as you can; math is the language of science, and the more math you know, the easier it is to do good research in any branch of science.
- Attend a college or university to earn a bachelor's or mas-

ter's degree in the type of science that most interests you.

- Look for internships to add more real-world experience to your skills before applying for a position.

Good luck, and have fun.

Honoring the Kraffts

After their deaths, Maurice and Katia Krafft were honored in many ways, in France and around the world.

- The Krafft Medal was established in 2004 by the International Association of Volcanology and Chemistry of the Earth's Interior (IAVCEI). It is awarded every four years to those who have made outstanding contributions to the volcanological community or to communities threatened by volcanic activity.
- The Katia and Maurice Krafft Award was established in 2018 by the European Geosciences Union. Each year it recognizes scientists who use innovative methods to inform diverse audiences about a geoscience topic or event.
- The Maurice and Katia Krafft Memorial Fund at the University of Hawai'i at Hilo helps volcanology students from other countries attend training courses at the university's Center for the Study of Active Volcanoes.
- Some elementary and middle schools in the Alsace region and elsewhere in France and on the island of Réunion are named after one or both of the Kraffts.
- The Maurice and Katia Krafft Complex in Wattwiller—the town where the Kraffts lived from 1976 to 1991—has a

meeting room, a theater, and a gymnastics hall.

- The Katia and Maurice Krafft Amphitheater is a lecture hall at the University of Strasbourg, where they studied and met.
- In Strasbourg and elsewhere in France, numerous streets are now named for one or both of the Kraffts.
- In 2022, two documentary films about the Kraffts were released: *Fire of Love*, directed by Sara Dosa, and *The Fire Within: A Requiem for Katia and Maurice Krafft*, directed by Werner Herzog.

The Krafft Medal, awarded by the International Association of Volcanology and Chemistry of the Earth's Interior. © IAVCEI.

Vulcania

Maurice and Katia had the idea for a volcano-themed amusement and educational park nestled among the extinct volcanic domes, craters, and crater lakes of the Chaîne des Puys in central France. When they were young, both of them had visited the area with their families. Official planning began after their deaths, and Vulcania opened in 2002. https://www.vulcania.com/en

La Cité du Volcan

With their friends who lived on the island of Réunion in the Indian Ocean, the Kraffts planned an interpretive center to educate the island's inhabitants and visitors about volcanoes around the world, and especially about Réunion's active volcano, Piton de la Fournaise. The original center, La Maison du Volcan (Volcano House) opened in 1992. The center was later renovated and enlarged, and it reopened in 2014 as La Cité du Volcan (Volcano City). It offers interactive exhibits, simulated volcanic environments, a theater, a lecture hall, and other amenities. From 2022 to 2024 it hosted a major exhibit about the Kraffts, thirty years after they died. https://museesreunion.fr/la-cite-du-volcan

Credit: Réunion des Musées Régionaux

Pele Dancing

Posters of one of the photos that Katia took of the lava flows on Mauna Loa on March 25, 1984, are available through the University of Hawai'i at Hilo. https://hilo.hawaii.edu/csav/krafft.php

Maurice's Dream

Maurice liked to say things that people would remember. Sometimes he was serious. Sometimes he was joking. And sometimes no one could be sure if he was joking or not. "I would like to make a canoe of titanium," Maurice said more than once. "And to go down the lava flow in a canoe, that must be fantastic—taking measurements [here] and taking measurements [there]. If we can find a company that wants to pay for the canoe, I want to go down the lava flow."

Further Resources

Books

Barone, Rebecca E. F. *Mountain of Fire: The Eruption and Survivors of Mount St. Helens*. New York: Henry Holt, 2024.

Jacobs, Robin. *Earth-Shattering Events*. London: Cicada, 2019.

Krafft, Maurice. *Volcanoes: Fire from the Earth*. New York: Abrams, 1993.

Lopes, Rosaly. *The Volcano Adventure Guide*. New York: Cambridge University Press, 2005.

Olson, Steve. *Eruption: The Untold Story of Mount St. Helens*. New York: W.W. Norton, 2016.

Rusch, Elizabeth. *Eruption! Volcanoes and the Science of Saving Lives*. New York: Houghton Mifflin Harcourt, 2013.

Scarth, Alwyn. *Vulcan's Fury: Man Against the Volcano*. New Haven, CT: Yale University Press, 1999.

Stewart, Melissa. *Inside Volcanoes*. New York: Sterling, 2011.

Van Rose, Susanna. *Eyewitness: Volcano and Earthquake*. New York: DK Publishing / Penguin Random House, 2022.

Winchester, Simon, and Dwight Jon Zimmerman. *The Day the World Exploded: The Earthshaking Catastrophe at Krakatoa*. New York: Collins, 2008.

Films

Dosa, Sara, director. *Fire of Love*. National Geographic Documentary Films, 2022, 98 min.

Herzog, Werner, director. *The Fire Within: A Requiem for Katia and Maurice Krafft*. Brian Leith Productions, 2022, 84 min.

Videos

Boyajian, Aram. *Volcano: Nature's Inferno*. Washington, DC: National Geographic Society, 2003.

Kelly, Ned. "The Volcano Watchers," an episode of *Nature*, PBS, 1987.

Websites

U.S. Geological Survey Volcano Hazards Program: https://www.usgs.gov/natural-hazards/volcano-hazards.

U.S. Geological Survey Volcanic Ashfall Impacts: https://www.usgs.gov/programs/VHP/ashfall-most-widespread-and-frequent-volcanic-hazard.

U.S. Volcano Disaster Assistance Program: https://volcanoes.usgs.gov/vdap/about.html.

Nevado del Ruiz—Remembering 1985: https://www.youtube.com/watch?v=lStwvwL8JRQ.

Short films about volcanic hazards, in many languages: https://vimeo.com/volfilm/videos.

Volcano World website at Oregon State University:
https://volcano.oregonstate.edu.

Smithsonian Institution's Global Volcanism Program
Information on historically active volcanoes around the world:
https://volcano.si.edu.
Reports of the most recent volcanic activity:
https://volcano.si.edu/reports_weekly.cfm.

Volcano Webcams

Kīlauea—Hawai'i, USA

https://www.usgs.gov/volcanoes/kilauea/webcams

Mount Augustine—Alaska, USA

https://avo.alaska.edu/volcano/Augustine
https://avo.alaska.edu/webcam

Mount Etna—Sicily, Italy

https://www.lave-volcans.com/lave_gp/index.php?action=051

Mount St. Helens—Washington, USA

https://www.usgs.gov/media/webcams/johnston-ridge-observatory-webcam-mount-st-helens

Others

https://webcams.volcanodiscovery.com

Selected Bibliography

Books

Conrad, Madeline. *Histoires d'une Passion: Maurice et Katia Krafft* (Stories of a Passion: Maurice and Katia Krafft). Colmar, France: Jérôme Do. Bentzinger Publishing, 2001 (in French).

de la Martinière, Hervé, ed. *Le Feu de la Terre: Katia et Maurice Krafft* (The Fire of the Earth: Katia and Maurice Krafft). Paris: Éditions de la Martinière, 1992 (in French).

Demaison, André. *Les Diables des Volcans: Maurice et Katia Krafft* (The Volcano Devils: Maurice and Katia Krafft). Grenoble, France: Éditions Glénat, 2011 (in French).

Doumas, Christos G. *Thera, Pompeii of the Ancient Aegean: Excavations at Akrotiri, 1967–1979*. London: Thames and Hudson, 1983.

Fearnley, Carina J., Deanne K. Bird, Katharine Haynes, William J. McGuire, and Gill Jolly, eds. *Observing the Volcano World: Volcano Crisis Communication*. Cham, Switzerland: Springer, 2018. Full book available online at: https://link.springer.com/book/10.1007/978-3-319-44097-2.

Fisher, Richard V. *Out of the Crater: Chronicles of a Volcanologist*. Princeton, NJ: Princeton University Press, 1999.

Fisher, Richard V., Grant Heiken, and Jeffrey B. Hulen. *Volcanoes: Crucibles of Change*. Princeton, NJ: Princeton University Press, 1997.

Furneaux, Rupert. *Krakatoa*. Englewood Cliffs, NJ: Prentice-Hall, 1964.

Gunnarsson, Arni. *Volcano: Ordeal by Fire in Iceland's Westmann Islands*. Reykjavik: Iceland Review Books, 1973.

Krafft, Katia, and Maurice Krafft. *Volcanoes: Earth's Awakening*. Maplewood, NJ: Hammond, 1980.

Krafft, Maurice, and Katia Krafft. *Volcano*. New York: Abrams, 1975.

Mather, Tamsin. *Adventures in Volcanoland: What Volcanoes Tell Us About the World and Ourselves*. Toronto: Hanover Square Press, 2024.

McPhee, John. "Cooling the Lava." In *The Control of Nature*. New York: Farrar Straus Giroux, 1989.

Newhall, Christopher G., and Raymundo S. Punongbayan, eds. *Fire and Mud: Eruptions and Lahars of Mount Pinatubo, Philippines*. Quezon City: Philippine Institute of Volcanology and Seismology and Seattle: University of Washington Press, 1996. Full book available online at https://pubs.usgs.gov/pinatubo/index.html.

Oppenheimer, Clive. *Eruptions That Shook the World*. Cambridge: Cambridge University Press, 2011.

Pálsson, Gísli. *Down to Earth: A Memoir*. Santa Barbara, CA: Punctum Books, 2020. Available online at https://punctumbooks.com/titles/down-to-earth.

Perret, Frank A. *The Eruption of Mt. Pelée, 1929–1932*. Carnegie Monograph Series 458. Washington, DC: Carnegie Institution of Washington, 1937.

Scarth, Alwyn. *Vulcan's Fury: Man Against the Volcano*. New Haven, CT: Yale University Press, 1999.

Scott, Kevin. *The Voice of This Stone: Learning from Volcanic Disasters Around the World*. Portland, OR: Carpe Diem Books, 2019.

Simkin, Tom, and Richard S. Fiske. *Krakatau 1883: The Volcanic Eruption and Its Effects*. Washington, D.C.: Smithsonian Institution Press, 1983.

Smith, Alan L., and M. John Roobol. *Mt. Pelée, Martinique; A Study of an Active Island-Arc Volcano*. Geological Society of America Memoir 175. Boulder, CO: Geological Society of America, 1990.

Tazieff, Haroun. *Nyiragongo: The Forbidden Volcano*. Woodbury, NY: Barron's, 1979.

Thompson, Dick. *Volcano Cowboys: The Rocky Evolution of a Dangerous Science*. New York: St. Martin's Press, 2000.

Vitaliano, Dorothy B. *Legends of the Earth*. Bloomington: Indiana University Press, 1973.

Waitt, Richard. *In the Path of Destruction: Eyewitness Chronicles of Mount St. Helens*. Pullman: Washington State University Press, 2014.

Westervelt, William D. *Hawaiian Legends of Volcanoes*. Rutland, VT: Charles E. Tuttle, 1963.

Williams, Stanley, and Fen Montaigne. *Surviving Galeras*. Boston: Houghton Mifflin Harcourt, 2001.

Winchester, Simon. *Krakatoa: The Day the World Exploded: August 27, 1883*. New York: HarperCollins, 2003.

Yanagi, Takeru, Hakuyu Okada, and Kazuya Ohta, eds. *Unzen Volcano: The 1990–1992 Eruption*. Fukuoka, Japan: Nishinippon Co. and Kyushu University Press, 1992.

Zeilinga de Boer, Jelle, and Donald Theodore Sanders. *Volcanoes in Human History: The Far-Reaching Effects of Major Eruptions*. Princeton, NJ: Princeton University Press, 2002.

Scientific Articles

Fisher, Richard V. "Decoupling of Pyroclastic Currents: Hazards Assessments." *Journal of Volcanology and Geothermal Research* 66 (1995): 257–63.

Glicken, Harry. "Rockslide-Debris Avalanche of May 18, 1980, Mount St. Helens Volcano, Washington." U.S. Geological Survey Open File Report 96-677 (1996).

Ishikawa, Yoshiharu, Takashi Yamada, and Shigemi Yajima. "A Study on the Pyroclastic Flows and Debris Flows Associated with the Mount Unzen Eruption in 1991." Public Works Research Institute Technical Memorandum No. 3141 (1992).

Keller, Jörg. "Memorial for Katja and Maurice Krafft." *Bulletin of Volcanology* 54, no. 7 (1992): 613–14.

Keller, Jörg, and Maurice Krafft, "Effusive Natrocarbonatite Activity of Oldoinyo Lengai, June 1988." *Bulletin of Volcanology* 52 (1990): 629–45.

Krafft, Maurice, and Jörg Keller. "Temperature Measurements in Carbonatite Lava Lakes and Flows from Oldoinyo Lengai, Tanzania." *Science* 245, no. 4914 (1989): 168–70.

Meara, Rhian H., Arnar Árnason, Osian H. Elias, Helga Hallbergsdóttir, and Sigurjón B. Hafsteinsson. "Magmatic Memories: Eldfell, 1973." Volcanica 7, no. 1 (2024): 361–403.

Nakada, Setsuya, and Toshitsugu Fujii. "Preliminary Report on the Activity at Unzen Volcano (Japan), November 1990–November 1991: Dacite Lava Domes and Pyroclastic Flows." *Journal of Volcanology and Geothermal Research* 54 (1993): 319–33.

Newhall, Chris, and Renato U. Solidum. "Volcanic Hazard Communication at Pinatubo from 1991 to 2015." In *Observing the Volcano World: Volcano Crisis Communication*, ed. Carina J. Fearnley, et al., Cham, Switzerland: Springer, 2018.

Sugimoto, Shinichi and Daisuke Nagai. "雲仙火山1991年6月3日の火砕流による人的被害" (Casualties by the 3 June 1991 Pyroclastic Flow at Unzen Volcano). 九大理研報　地球惑星 (Kyushu University Research Institute Report, Earth and Planetary Science) 22, no. 3 (2009): 9–22 (in Japanese).

Yamamoto, Takahiro, Shinji Takarada, and Shigeru Suto, "Pyroclastic Flows from the 1991 Eruption of Unzen Volcano, Japan." *Bulletin of Volcanology* 55 (1993): 166–75.

Videos

Krafft, Maurice, producer. *Understanding Volcanic Hazards*. IAVCEI (International Association of Volcanology and Chemistry of the Earth's Interior), 1991, 1995, and 2009, 25 min.

Magazines

Francis, Peter, and Stephen Self. "The Eruption of Krakatau." *Scientific American*, November 1983, 172.

Grove, Noel. "A Village Fights for Its Life." *National Geographic*, July 1973, 40–67.

McDowell, Bart. "Eruption in Colombia." *National Geographic*, May 1986, 640–53.

Rosen, Julia. "Benchmarks: May 8, 1902: The Deadly Eruption of Mount Pelée." *Earth*, April 2015. https://www.earthmagazine.org/article/benchmarks-may-8-1902-deadly-eruption-mount-pelee; accessed on November 10, 2023.

Thomas, Lately. "Prelude to Doomsday." *American Heritage*, August 1961. https://www.americanheritage.com/prelude-doomsday; accessed on November 12, 2023.

Websites

"1973-Allir í bátana" (Everyone in the boats), *Soegurnar* (*Stories*). 1973-alliribatana.com; https://en.1973-alliribatana.com/soegurnar; accessed on November 28, 2023 (in Icelandic).

Atlas Obscura. "The Prison Cell of Ludger Sylbaris, Saint-Pierre, Martinique," atlasobscura.com, 2013. https://www.atlasobscura.com/places/the-prison-cell-of-ludger-sylbaris-saint-pierre-martinique; accessed on November 12, 2023.

Cullen-Tanaka, Janet. "Interview with Maurice and Katia Krafft." Originally published in *Volcano Quarterly*, January 1992; reprinted online at now-defunct Volcano World website of University of North Dakota. Archived online at https://archive.li/JcCeL; accessed on August 1, 2018.

El-Hai, Jack. "The Short and Wondrous Career of Harry Glicken." Medium.com, December 7, 2017. https://medium.com/@Jack_ElHai/the-short-and-wondrous-career-of-harry-glicken-7a1d310ed3d8; accessed on November 25, 2018.

Global Volcanism Program. "Report on Pinatubo (Philippines)." *Bulletin of the Global Volcanism Network* 16, no. 5 (1991). Washington, DC: Smithsonian Institution. https://doi.org/10.5479/si.GVP.BGVN199105-273083.

Global Volcanism Program. "Report on Unzendake (Japan)." *Bulletin of the Global Volcanism Network* 16, no. 5 (1991). Washington, DC: Smithsonian Institution. https://doi.org/10.5479/si.GVP.BGVN199105-282100.

Hug-Fleck, Christof. “Expediton zum kältesten Vulkane—Eine Reportage” (Expedition to the Coldest Volcano—A Report), 1988. Vulkane.net. https://www.vulkane.net/reportagen/lengai/1988.html; accessed on September 2, 2018 (in German).

Lefebvre, Thierry. “L’éruption du cinéma: Aux sources des *Rendez-vous du Diable*” (The eruption of cinema: At the sources of the *Rendez-vous du Diable*). *1895* 39 (online) (2003). http://journals.openedition.org/1895/3202; accessed on November 25, 2018 (in French).

NOVA. “Deadly Shadow of Vesuvius—Interview with C. Dan Miller of the VDAP Team,” 1998. http://www.pbs.org/wgbh/nova/vesuvius/team.html; accessed on June 28, 2010.

Acknowledgments

My heartfelt thanks go out to the many people who helped me over the course of this project:

The many teachers whose lessons—intentional or otherwise—informed me about volcanoes and their activity.

All those whose memories of the Kraffts, or accounts of their own encounters with volcanoes from 1883 till now, were important to telling this story.

The volcanologists around the world who publish the results of their research so others can build on it and discover even more.

The experts and specialists who reviewed portions of the manuscript or provided photographs, including Jonathan Fink, PhD, Portland State University and University of British Columbia; Michael Poland, PhD, United States Geological Survey; Ulrich Kueppers, PhD, IAVCEI Secretary General; and Claude Grandpey, honorary president of L'Association Volcanologique Européenne (L.A.V.E.).

Danny Meldung, who wrangled photo permissions.

My agent, Ammi-Joan Paquette, who found the perfect editor for this story.

My editor, Kate O'Sullivan, who recognized that my short original manuscript might actually be simply a seed that could grow into something much more.

HarperCollins team members, including Alison Klapthor, Heather Tamarkin, Alison Kerr Miller, Mary Magrisso, Melissa Cicchitelli, Emily Mannon, Samantha Brown, Ellen Fast, Mimi Rankin, and Patty Rosati, who turned my words into the real book you're holding in your hands.

Katherine Roy, who brought Katia and Maurice to life in her dynamic illustrations.

My writing group, which has provided invaluable advice and many enjoyable Wednesday evenings: Laurie Ann Thompson, Lois Brandt, Dan Richards, Dori Hillestad Butler, Kevan Atteberry, Vikram Madan, Joni Sensel, Jeanie Mebane, Allyson Schrier, Lisa L. Owens, and Dana Sullivan.

And my family: my wife Becky, daughter Frances, and cat Felix (always more interested in a warm lap than in rocks).